Praise

"A must-read for our uncertain times. Army veteran EJ Snyder hits the ground running, delivering this masterful survival guide into the hands of the common man. Drawing from his 25-year military career, combined with over a decade of expertise as a survival instructor and a television survival adventure personality, EJ has done the work for you in this step-by-step, chapter-by-chapter instructional guide. Simply read and prepare."

—Shawn Kelly, creator of Corporals Corner, survival instructor, and YouTube personality

"As a colleague of EJ Snyder for over a decade, I've witnessed firsthand his unwavering dedication to engagement in the art of survival. With twenty-five years of military service under his belt, including specialized training in survival tactics, as well as various extreme Media projects, EJ's expertise is unmatched. Now, with the release of this comprehensive guidebook, EJ brings together his wealth of experience to offer an organized roadmap for survival that is both practical and inclusive. From shelter and water procurement to self-defense and morale maintenance, each chapter is crafted to be implemented by everyone, from novices to seasoned pros. What truly sets this guide apart is EJ's commitment to inclusivity. He has meticulously crafted this book to ensure that regardless of background or means, everyone can benefit from its wisdom. In uncertain times, this book serves as a vital tool for empowerment, offering the knowledge and skills necessary to navigate any challenge. With EJ Snyder as your guide, you can embark on a transformative journey toward self-reliance and resilience. Prepare to face the unknown fortified with the wisdom of a true survivalist."

—Cat Bigney, survival consultant and anthropologist

"EJ has an extensive background in not only survival (military and civilian) but also in educating, mentoring and motivational speaking. Through personal experience, classroom education and self-discovery, EJ has become one of the most prolific survivalists in the world. Not only does he survive in the wilderness, but also in today's ever-changing and sometimes frightening landscape of urban and suburban turmoil. Are you curious? Do you feel fear creep in when you watch the evening

news? Do you wonder if you would be able to protect your family in an emergency? Would you actually know what to do when faced with an unavoidable nefarious event? Do you ever wake up in the middle of the night and wonder, 'what if'? If any of these thoughts run through your mind, then this is the book that you won't be able to put down. It certainly was for me."

—Wes Harper, "The Assassin", survivalist and author
of *Killin' It in the Kitchen*

EMERGENCY HOME PREPAREDNESS

EMERGENCY HOME PREPAREDNESS

THE ULTIMATE GUIDE FOR BUGGING IN DURING NATURAL DISASTERS, PANDEMICS, CIVIL UNREST, AND MORE

EJ SNYDER

AND THE SURVIVAL SUMMIT
WWW.EJSNYDER.COM

Skyhorse Publishing

Skyhorse Publishing books may be purchased in bulk at special discounts for sales promotion, corporate gifts, fund-raising, or educational purposes. Special editions can also be created to specifications. For details, contact the Special Sales Department, Skyhorse Publishing, 307 West 36th Street, 11th Floor, New York, NY 10018 or info@skyhorsepublishing.com.

Skyhorse® and Skyhorse Publishing® are registered trademarks of Skyhorse Publishing, Inc.®, a Delaware corporation.

Visit our website at www.skyhorsepublishing.com.

Please follow our publisher Tony Lyons on Instagram @tonylyonsisuncertain.

10 9 8 7 6 5 4 3 2 1

Library of Congress Cataloging-in-Publication Data is available on file.

Print ISBN: 978-1-5107-7954-9
Ebook ISBN: 978-1-5107-7955-6

Cover design by Kai Texel
Cover photo credit by The Survival Summit

Printed in China

TABLE OF CONTENTS

INTRODUCTION

We are living in uncertain and dangerous times. We are faced with pandemics, natural disasters, civil unrest, and even war, and you need to be ready for such events. I am EJ Snyder, an extreme survivalist and a twenty-five-year Army combat vet. I am bringing my years of knowledge and experience to help you in these situations. You have probably seen me on television on *Naked and Afraid*, *Dual Survival*, and *First Man Out*, but I am more than just a wilderness survivalist. I am a total survivalist, and that means my skills apply here at home too.

The critical information in this book could save you and your loved ones' lives. Some tips included are how to prepare a get-home bag, how to set up your vehicle, and getting yourself home in an emergency. Once you get home, I will teach you the framework of how to set up your residence to be prepared to "bug in." "Bugging in" refers to the strategic choice of staying put in your primary residence or a predetermined safe location during a significant event or natural disaster, as opposed to evacuating or "bugging out" to a different location. This approach involves preparing in advance by stockpiling essential supplies such as water, food, medical kits, and other necessities to sustain yourself and your family members for an extended period. The rationale behind bugging in is to utilize the familiar surroundings and resources of your home, where you may feel safer and more secure. It requires comprehensive planning, including ensuring your home is fortified against potential threats and having a communication plan in place. This strategy is favored when the home offers a safe haven and when moving to another location poses greater risks. We will review bugging in vs. bugging out, PACE planning, EDC (everyday carry) considerations, emergency communications, vehicle preparedness, setting up caches, community and networking, and much more.

This book is specifically crafted to cater to individuals from all walks of life. Whether you reside in a bustling metropolis or a serene rural area, regardless of your personal background, circumstances, or financial means, this comprehensive guide serves as the blueprint for preparing yourself for an array of potential scenarios. From the essentials to the intricacies, I'm going to share with you a ton of tips and advice on how to get your home ready for any situation.

Before delving into the specifics of this invaluable resource, providing you with some insights into my own journey is essential. I will share with you the experiences that set me on the path to survivalism. A significant chapter of my life unfolded within the military, where I honed my skills and developed a profound understanding of preparedness in the face of adversity. Along this trajectory, I found myself embracing thrilling adventures on popular survival-based television programs, such as the renowned series *Naked and Afraid*.

In this book, I weave together tales of personal growth, military service, and stories from the realm of survivalist entertainment. Let me be your guide as we begin a transformative journey toward self-reliance and the acquisition of lifesaving knowledge. Together, we will delve into the depths of practical skills, mental fortitude, and the resilience required to confront any challenge that may come our way.

Within the pages of this book, you will discover a comprehensive array of essential survival techniques and valuable insights derived from my own experiences. From basic necessities to advanced strategies, we will traverse the vast landscape of home preparedness, leaving no stone unturned. Through storytelling, practical advice, and step-by-step instructions, I am committed to empowering you with the tools necessary to thrive amid uncertainty.

Prepare to unlock your potential, embrace the adventurer within, and go on an awe-inspiring expedition of knowledge and self-discovery. Together, let us start this remarkable literary odyssey as we uncover the secrets of survival, resilience, and the indomitable human spirit.

The Early Years

I grew up in a tough Italian neighborhood in northern New Jersey, just outside New York City. Over the years, I learned many outdoor skills and greatly loved the wilderness. My father took my late kid brother Jeff and me camping, hiking, hunting, fishing, and trapping quite often, and it was the freest I had ever felt while out in the wilderness. There is something deeply inspiring about being a part of nature and learning to live off the land the way our ancestors did, and what I found early on was that this leads to a lot of personal inner growth, an evolution of oneself, and great self-confidence. I also found a Zen-like peace and calmness in nature. My connection to the outdoors started at a very young age, and it has stuck with me ever since. It truly became a basis of my character and helped form who I'd become through my life's journey.

Anytime I could get in the woods, I did, and I joined scouting as a way to be there. I was not the kid interested in selling popcorn, participating in pine derby races, or collecting litter in parks—I wanted to be in the wilderness. I grew up in the concrete jungle but felt so out of place and out of sorts. I had difficulties adapting. I learned early on that mindset was everything in life, from all of the time I spent in the woods as a child, throughout my military career, and later in life surviving all over the world in some of the most extreme places on earth.

My brother and I furthered our skills by canoeing, rafting, rock climbing, and taking long extended hikes. We could often be found near the nearest set of woods or waterways within the confines of the concrete jungle.

I remember being out in the woods one year hunting with my dad in upstate New York in the early winter when I was eight. It was cold and snowy, and we had walked out to our afternoon spot and sat down, waiting. The temperature had dropped significantly, I was beginning to freeze, and heavy snow started falling. My dad told me to head back to the lodge, retracing our tracks. So off I went. I was moving along well, but the tracks were now covered entirely, and darkness fell. Long story short, I became lost and was scared and half-frozen by the time my dad and uncle found me. After that, I knew I had to learn my way in the wild or perish by it. I constantly paid extra attention, asked questions, and practiced all the skills I learned.

My brother and I experienced a lot together in the outdoors. We did many crazy things and pushed the envelope to the extreme. We would free-climb cliffs in New Jersey off the Delaware River, in upstate New York, and in Vermont tied to just each other; hit white water rivers in blow-up rafts; and do other insane "Momma Said Not To!" things. We were known as very wild and untamed kids.

Among the many chapters that make up my life, there is one marked by deep sorrow: the death of my brother before his twenty-second birthday. The profound loss I experienced at that moment left an indelible mark on my soul. The days that followed were shrouded in a haze of sorrow, each breath a poignant reminder of the absence that would forever define my existence.

Yet, I find solace and strength in the memories we crafted together in the wilderness. Those precious moments spent side

by side, surrounded by the serene beauty of the natural world, have become the cornerstone of my existence. He continues to guide me, an eternal compass pointing toward a life of purpose and reverence for the natural world.

I have learned to cherish the memories of my brother as precious treasures. They serve as beacons of light, illuminating my path even in the darkest of moments. The wilderness, once our sanctuary of shared experiences, has now become a sanctuary of solace and remembrance—a space where our connection continues to exist.

I carry the lessons learned in the wilderness with me. They have shaped my perspective, instilled in me a profound appreciation for the world around me, and fueled a passionate dedication to preserving nature's fragile harmony.

Military Career

Dedicated to the call of duty, I spent twenty-five years of my life serving in the United States Army, undertaking leading roles within Infantry and Airborne units, specifically as a Ranger. A mere nineteen years old when I first donned the uniform, I embarked on a journey that would shape the course of my existence.

Rapidly ascending the ranks, I swiftly gained valuable experience and insights. The crucible of combat beckoned during the Gulf War in 1991, followed by a grueling fifteen-month tour during Operation Iraqi Freedom from 2004 to 2005. Through these harrowing experiences I truly understood the magnitude of sacrifice and the commitment demanded by our great nation. In recognition of my unwavering dedication, I was honored with two Bronze Star Medals, the Legion of Merit, the Order of St. Maurice (Centurion), and a collection of over forty other medals and decorations.

I received my first formal training in survival at the illustrious U.S. Army Ranger School, an experience that reignited the flames of fascination of my youth. Driven by an insatiable hunger for knowledge, I embarked on an immersive self-study expedition, voraciously absorbing as many survival techniques as I could possibly grasp.

My deep passion propelled me forward, and destiny intervened when I was assigned as a Ranger instructor, affording me the opportunity to further enhance my skill set by attending the U.S. Army Survival School (SERE-C) and Tracking Course. In a remarkable turn of events, I assumed the role of primary survival and tracking instructor, igniting a lifelong dedication to sharing my expertise with others.

My service in the Army was marked by a never-ending pursuit of excellence. Embracing a relentless pursuit of knowledge and skill, I eagerly sought opportunities to expand my repertoire through attendance at various specialized schools. These endeavors not only bolstered my expertise but also provided me with the unique opportunity to deploy on diverse training and missions worldwide. Throughout my career, I found myself honored with numerous accolades and commendations, a testament to my steadfast commitment and performance.

Throughout my military journey, I fulfilled multiple roles, including that of a Ranger instructor, survival and tracking instructor, and drill sergeant. My indomitable spirit and unyielding determination earned me the moniker "Skullcrusher," a tribute to my status as both a standout athlete and a powerful combatant, and, well, in all honesty, a barracks party gone awry may have aided a little, too. Climbing the ranks, I retired with honor as a Sergeant Major / E-9, embodying the epitome of leadership and commitment.

After the Army

After leaving the Army, I transitioned into a role as a government contractor, imparting my extensive survival skills and knowledge to future Green Berets and other soldiers at the U.S. Army SERE School. A strong believer in the transformative power of survivalist education, I remain steadfast in my commitment to instilling these crucial skills in soldiers and civilians alike. For over three decades, I have diligently shared my expertise, equipping others with the tools to survive and thrive, whether in the wilderness or amid the chaos of combat.

Rooted in an unyielding resolve and fortified by the lessons learned throughout my career, I continue to live by the motto Tua Sponte Superstes, Latin for "survive by your own will." My passion for survival skills remains undiminished, and I find immeasurable fulfillment in the act of sharing this knowledge with others.

Television

After my time in the Army, I found myself contemplating retirement and pondering what the next chapter of my life would hold. I realized that it was the perfect moment to revive an old dream I had long harbored—a desire to immerse myself in the world of entertainment in some capacity. With a leap of faith, I decided to explore the realm of TV and film, both as a military technical adviser and as a participant in stunt work and acting.

Fortune favored my endeavors as I swiftly found success within the industry. Opportunities in mainstream films, television shows, commercials, web series, and independent and student film projects beckoned, allowing me to showcase my talents. It was my role as "Redfern," a freighter boat mercenary, in the hit TV series *Lost* that garnered significant recognition, propelling me further into the spotlight. Notable projects such as the History Channel's *Patton 360* and the Chiller Network's *Can You Survive a Horror Movie?* followed suit, solidifying my presence in the realm of TV and film.

Soon, I found myself being recruited for prominent reality competition shows, emerging as a finalist for *Survivor 21* and *Big Brother 14*. The intersection of my real-world survival skills and television finally materialized when I embarked on TNT's *72 Hours: The Fijian Jungle* (episode 7).

In due course, I embarked on the filming of the pilot episode of *Naked and Afraid: Terror in Tanzania*. This twenty-one-day survival challenge involved two strangers, a man and a woman, coming together completely naked with a single item each to survive until extraction three weeks later. I proudly emerged as the first man to complete the challenge. The item I had in Tanzania was a K-Bar Tanto edge combat knife. This knife actually broke due to my rugged use, though it was still functional, just degraded. The lesson was when it comes to gear and survival situations, second best will not cut it when your life depends on it. It propelled me to search for the best survival knife out there that could be a one-tool option. They said it didn't exist, and I found many good options but they were right. . . . A one-tool option seemed like a unicorn. So, I decided to fix that problem and design a knife with TOPS Knives that would fit this calling, and the SXB (Skullcrusher Extreme Blade) was born. Seven months later, I was joined by Laura Zerra in *Naked and Afraid: Man vs. Amazon*, conquering the twenty-one-day challenge once again, thus solidifying my title as the first man to complete it twice. Subsequently, I received an invitation to participate in the forty-day challenge of *Naked and Afraid XL* in the Colombian Badlands, making me the only man to complete the challenge three times. Recently, I had the honor of cohosting the ninth season of *Dual Survival* alongside my *Naked and Afraid XL* partner, Jeff Zausch.

Jeff and I tested our skills and partnership in various harsh locations, navigating unforgiving environments and confronting challenging situations. From Brazil and South Africa to Utah's High Desert and the swamplands of Louisiana, we pushed ourselves to the limits of human endurance. We even found ourselves in a cave in the former USSR state of Georgia and braved the tumultuous events of the Turkish coup while at the Istanbul Airport.

In 2019, I was once again called upon to take on another *Naked and Afraid* challenge, this time going solo in *Naked and Afraid ALONE: Lonely Like the Wolf*. I ventured into the Balkan Mountains of Bulgaria, unaware that three others were simultaneously taking on the challenge on the other side of the mountain. After twenty-one days of being stalked by wolves, enduring freezing conditions, and battling hunger, I stood atop the 5,500-foot extraction site, triumphantly emerging as the sole survivor of the Balkan Mountains. Thus, I earned the moniker "The Beast of Bulgaria."

Next, I set out to be on the *Naked and Afraid: Legends* challenge in the treacherous Atchafalaya Basin of Louisiana. Despite encountering a life-threatening injury halfway through the sixty-day challenge—a tear that required stitches in the field without the luxury of pain medication—I persevered and finished the grueling endeavor. This experience solidified my status as a legend, showcasing my determination and resilience in the face of adversity.

But my journey was far from over. I couldn't resist the call of the Amazon, returning to the exact location I had ventured to in 2013, eight years later. While others succumbed once again to the challenges posed by the unforgiving Amazon jungle, I stepped in to lend a helping hand. This time, I endured another forty-three days, adding to my tally of survival feats. With a total of 206 Naked Survival Days under my belt, I proudly carry the title of "The Godfather of *Naked and Afraid*."

Beyond my television appearances, I have expanded my horizons further, embarking on exciting ventures in the entertainment industry. I am thrilled to serve as the cohost of the great new series *Mountain Masters* on the Inspire Network, where we explore the breathtaking wonders of mountainous landscapes. Additionally, I have collaborated with the Mr. Beast YouTube channel, creating engaging video content that captivates and entertains audiences worldwide.

As I reflect upon my journey thus far, I am filled with gratitude for the remarkable opportunities that have come my way. From my humble beginnings in the Army to unforgettable experiences in the realm of survival and entertainment, each chapter has shaped me into the person I am today. It is my passion for survival skills, the unyielding spirit of adventure, and the genuine desire to inspire others that continue to fuel my drive.

Teaching Survival Skills

In the years following my retirement, I have dedicated myself wholeheartedly to the mission of imparting survival skills to a wide range of individuals. From seasoned soldiers seeking to enhance their expertise to civilians yearning for self-reliance, my commitment to sharing knowledge knows no bounds. Through my teaching endeavors, I have observed the transformative power of survival education, witnessing individuals evolve from novices to confident and capable practitioners of self-preservation.

Guided by the wisdom acquired through years of military service, I have refined my instructional techniques, blending practicality, theory, and hands-on experience to create a comprehensive learning environment. It is my fervent belief that survival skills are not merely tools for the wilderness but vital life skills that foster adaptability, resourcefulness, and the ability to overcome obstacles in any scenario.

Through my courses, students are exposed to a wealth of practical exercises and immersive simulations that test their mettle and expand their capabilities. From building shelters and foraging for sustenance to navigation techniques and emergency medical care, each aspect of survival is meticulously explored. With an emphasis on situational awareness, risk assessment, and decision-making under pressure, I instill in my students the resilience and mental fortitude required to thrive in even the most adverse circumstances.

Looking ahead, I eagerly embrace the future, ready to tackle new challenges, embark on daring adventures, and share my expertise with the world. With every step I take, I am reminded of the indomitable human spirit, capable of triumphing over seemingly insurmountable odds. As I navigate uncharted territories, both in the wild and in the realm of entertainment, I remain committed to pushing the boundaries of what is possible and inspiring others to do the same.

The journey is far from over, and I invite you to join me on this exhilarating expedition. Together, let us unlock the untapped potential within ourselves, embrace the thrill of the unknown, and discover the extraordinary within the ordinary.

CHAPTER 1

WHAT IS HOME PREPAREDNESS, OR "BUGGING IN"?

What Is "Bugging In"?

A survival or emergency situation can happen anytime, anywhere, with anyone. In most cases, you will only be able to use what you have on and around you. If the COVID-19 pandemic has taught me one big thing, it is that probably 95 percent of the world is going to "bug in," and the very few who are "bugging out" are only going somewhere to "bug in" anyways.

So, fully understanding what "bugging in" is, how it is done, and all the particulars are super important. Even if you are set up for something as extreme as the apocalypse, you can rest easy when a hurricane comes to your neighborhood, because you know you will be ready for anything.

You might be asking yourself what "bugging in" means. Bugging in is when you have decided that the situation you have found yourself in is terrible, and that you need to get home as fast as possible to hunker down and weather the "storm."

You could be hunkering down because there is an actual storm, out-of-control civil unrest in your area, a dangerous pandemic, a massive solar flare that took down a large portion of the US electrical grid, or even a world war. Whatever the situation, you need to be ready to provide for all your needs for as long as you might have to stay at your primary location.

In the introduction of this book, I mentioned "PACE planning." If you are not familiar with this acronym, PACE stands for: P = primary, A = alternate, C = contingency, and E = emergency. Your primary "bug-in" location is your residence. Your alternate may be a neighbor's or a friend's house. Your contingency could be a family member's home in a more rural area, and your emergency location, God forbid, might be somewhere in the wilderness, preferably on state land, so you are not intruding on someone else's property. That is a good way to get yourself shot.

Why should you bug in as opposed to bug out? Well, that is a big question that probably many of you are asking, and the answer is relatively simple. Most of society will not be ready to bug out and live in the wilderness. It takes a certain mindset, tenacity, skill set, training, and endurance to live out in the wild for an extended time. It should also be the drop-dead last-ditch plan you implement, which is why it is the emergency in your overall PACE plan.

Even if you have caches along specific routes for resupply, and the supplies and gear to bug out into the wilderness, do not make that the primary location. When bugging in at home, you will have general supplies there, and physically and mentally, you will feel much safer. Psychologically it is a better starting point as well, as you will feel more in control and confident in your situation.

Now, there may be circumstances where you cannot make it home, or your home has been struck by a natural disaster, such as a flood or fire. If this is the case, you should plan to bug in at your alternate location, which should be preplanned and rehearsed as often as possible. Just like you should be practicing fire drills with your family regularly, or going over earthquake drills if you live somewhere like California, you should be doing the same regarding your individual PACE plans.

PACE Plan Example

John Doe and his family live in the United States Northwest, Washington State, in a small home in a relatively quiet suburban neighborhood. John and his family have a readily available supply of emergency food storage, a backup generator, and plenty of emergency preparedness supplies. The primary location in John's PACE plan is their home. In an emergency, John and his family will meet at their home to hunker down.

PACE

- PRIMARY
- ALTERNATE
- CONTINGENCY
- EMERGENCY

John recognizes that situations such as wildfires or other natural disasters could force his family out of their primary location. There could also be issues with civil unrest in John's area. John has recognized the fact that leaving his primary location could become an eventuality, so John has spoken with a friend of his in another neighborhood close by about using their property as their alternate location. John has coordinated with his neighbor to ensure that if the need arises, he and his family can go to his friend's location, and he has kept some supplies at this neighbor's home.

The next step in John's PACE plan is the contingency plan. John's contingency plan is to drive two hours south to a relative's house in a more remote location. John and his family would relocate to this property if his primary and alternate plans could not be enacted for reasons out of his control.

John has placed a couple of supply caches along the route to his contingency location in case his vehicle becomes disabled and his family must finish the trip on foot. John has also coordinated with the contingency locations to have basic supplies on hand for his family.

If all of John's plans become unavailable, his last-ditch emergency plan is to have each family member gather their bug-out bags and go to their predetermined location deep in the forest, on state land. John does not plan to live out in the forest for the rest of their lives. This is simply a temporary solution to the problem of having his primary, alternate, and contingency plans fall apart.

John's situation might make it dangerous for his family to go into town for a while, so they may have to temporarily stay at their emergency bug-out location until things settle down. John made sure that he had supply caches pre-staged at his emergency site in case they are forced to leave their contingency location faster than they had planned.

The example of John Doe was a particular case. Please keep in mind that everyone's situation is going to be different. I will not discuss specific PACE plans and locations in this book besides the example I gave about "John Doe" because every person and every family will have a different strategy based on their particular needs.

What I am going to do is lay out is the framework necessary to provide for your needs and your family's needs. Our primary needs are security, shelter, fire, water filtration, power alternatives, medical supplies, food storage, emergency communications, and land navigation in case you find yourself far from home without transportation or need to use unfamiliar alternate routes.

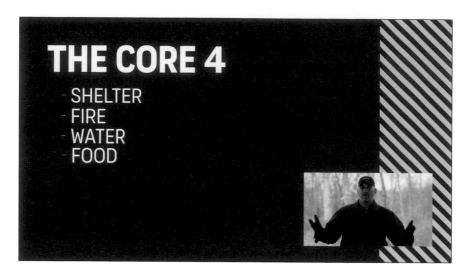

THE CORE 4
- SHELTER
- FIRE
- WATER
- FOOD

If you are not at home when disaster strikes, you may be unable to rely on your cell phone to use Google Maps to find your way home. It would be best if you had a street map in your vehicle and topographical (topo) maps of your area. You may find yourself traveling on foot and need to travel through wooded areas to get yourself home.

Another factor could be that you live in a larger city, and you are worried about being trapped in the city if there are significant blackouts or major civil unrest, which is a legitimate concern. Depending on the exact situation, staying in the city may be the worst for you or your family, and you may need to fall back to one of your alternate locations immediately. These preplanned locations should be a part of your overall PACE plan. You never know how quickly you may need to escape your primary area, so you and your family must be ready if you need to flee.

When getting home from work, school, or another location, do you know how many hours or days it might take you to get home? How long in a vehicle versus on foot? The same questions will apply if you must get to an alternate location. These are all details you should consider planning and training. Everyone in your family should be on the same page in knowing what to do in an emergency.

When it comes to getting back home or to an alternate or contingency location, it is likely impossible to know what you may need to do because we cannot predict the future. We do not know what the situation might be, so there are many things to consider. You may need a complete survival gear kit and security items such as a firearm and a knife.

You must ensure you have everything you need to get home or get out of Dodge for a day, a couple of days, or even longer. What about those with you or at home: your loved ones, your wife, girlfriend, husband, boyfriend, or your kids? What do they have? Do they each have their readily available preparedness gear?

PROS OF BUGGING-IN
- EASIER THAN BUGGING-OUT
- ACCESS TO MORE SUPPLIES/RESOURCES
- PHYSICALLY + PSYCHOLOGICALLY SAFER
- ACCOMODATES YOUNG, INFIRM, + DISABLED

CHAPTER 2

GETTING HOME

EDC (Everyday Carry)

You must always be ready for whatever comes your way. My step-dad always used to say, "expect the unexpected." That has stuck with me all my life. When I was in school, there were many problems. Kids grew up in the wrong environment where crime, drugs, and violence were all around us. That always affected the school or the neighborhood, with gangs trying to run things, jumping other kids they did not like, muggings in the bathroom, and robberies. So, I always walked around ready for anything. I would carry rolls of quarters in my pocket, carry a switchblade, and wear steel-toe boots. I did not want to be a victim, and to make sure that did not happen, I stayed ready. Looking back now, EDC was a part of my life and ensured I always made it home safely.

EDC stands for Everyday Carry. EDC gear would be the things you have on your person, such as your phone, a lighter, a choice of a folding knife, a pocketknife, and or multi-tool that you carry on your belt. Some folks carry smaller flat fixed blades in a sheath, a firearm, and maybe even some escape and evasion gear, such as hidden handcuff keys, a lockpick set, and Kevlar cordage to

escape from zip ties, duct tape, and other nonmetal bindings, in case you ever find yourself in a terrible situation.

Before we get into bugging in at your home, we first need to get you there. Let's discuss the most obvious scenarios, such as if you are at work, or you are at school, or just out shopping or eating at your favorite restaurant. You could be on vacation, or at a function like a family event, a charity fundraiser, or a sporting event—anywhere! Wherever you may be on any given day, we need to get you from point A to point B as quickly and safely as possible. How will you get to where you need to be and do it safely and have some survival items to make it easier? Again, it can start with something as simple as a checklist. As an avid survivalist, it is not uncommon for me to have covered all my bases and multiple setups.

Whatever you can comfortably carry on your person is considered your EDC gear, but what if you wear a suit to work? You may not be able to carry very much on your person. Whether or not you have a robust EDC setup, you should also have a backpack or another pack where you keep your "bug-out" bag, or as some like to call it, your "get home" bag.

There are a lot of different names out there on the internet. Still, it all boils down to having the necessary gear you need to survive while trying to get to your primary or alternate location and ensuring that all your needs are covered for at least a couple of days if necessary. So, you can call this bag or pack whatever you want, if you understand what should be in it.

"Get to Your Car" Gear List

These items will aid you in getting to your vehicle, keeping you safe, and making the situation more manageable. You probably are not going that far, but if civil unrest is occurring with riots and bad actors taking advantage of the problem, a mile can seem like ten miles. In any case, this is a good starting point to cover here and consider.

- One-gallon ziplock bag
- EDC knife (can be your choice to help with tasks like a pocketknife, multi-tool, or regular fixed blade or folder, which can also be used in defense)
- Water container (preferably one that filters or purifies water, or a steel canteen in which you can boil water). Recommended stainless steel containers are 32–40 ounces. Water purifiers, such as the Grayl GeoPress, are 24 ounces, and can be used to store water.
- Water purification tablets, water filters, or other means to purify
- Fire starter or lighter
- Small flashlight and/or headlamp with extra batteries
- Compass
- Emergency blanket and poncho (these are small and compactly packaged and can act as temporary shelter and protect your core body temp)
- Raincoat (great asset to keep you dry and warm)
- Small tarp and fifty feet of paracord
- Snack food (jerky sticks, granola bars, trail mix)
- Small first aid kit with pain meds and prescriptions
- Communication needs, cell phone, small portable radio, walkie-talkie
- Additional self-defense items to protect you (maybe a walking stick, small club, mace, pepper spray, Taser, etc.)
- Firearm for protection (local, state, and federal laws apply here)
- Escape and evasion gear, such as lockpick sets, handcuff keys, Kevlar cordage, etc.

Being the "Gray Man"

The "gray man" theory is a strategy that has proven indispensable in my survival experiences across various environments—be it bustling streets, treacherous combat zones, or the unforgiving wilderness. At its core, being a "gray man" entails the art of seamlessly blending into your surroundings, becoming virtually indistinguishable from the ordinary individuals that populate your environment.

One such occasion was when I was in Iraq. We were after a high-priority targeted individual and were getting very good intel on his movements and activities. We received a critical tip one day about a meeting that was supposed to happen, and we were told the target was to be present at this location. The issue was the place where the meeting was to happen was in the middle of the city near a marketplace.

We needed to know that it was positively him, that he had arrived and was inside the building, and what threats were with him in the form of enemy combatants, how many, types of weapons, and position. This required us to send in a few men to have eyes on the objective. I grabbed my interpreter and two additional soldiers and met our contact at the city's edge.

We had moved soldiers into position the night before in buildings to wait for the assault to go down. We made radio contact with all the strike teams and moved ourselves into a position which was in a market stand across the street from the building we needed eyes on. We were only armed with pistols but had AK-47s hidden under the market table.

We were dressed in local garb with head wraps and face coverings, and I wore sunglasses to hide my blue eyes. We had rigged SAPI plates (body armor protection) underneath our clothes. The market was bustling so we blended in nicely as we easily moved into position and waited. The hour arrived and we could easily see the target. He suspected nothing and went into the building with the three men he had accompanying him with only two visible AKs. We radioed to alert all strike team units to get ready. After several minutes we called in the signal and all units moved in. The target and his men were all taken by surprise and captured.

Achieving this feat requires the cultivation of exceptional situational awareness, a heightened state of alertness that enables you to comprehend the nuances of your surroundings and be attuned to the ever-changing dynamics unfolding around you. This skill, honed over years of practice, has been a cornerstone of my survival journey, serving as a shield that has safeguarded me from harm's way time and time again.

When considering the physical attributes that contribute to the "gray man" persona, it is crucial to be mindful of the subtle nuances that can make all the difference in maintaining a low profile. While some situations may warrant the use of a military-style backpack equipped with MOLLE attachments, drawing attention to yourself in such a manner may not always be advisable.

MOLLE stands for modular lightweight load-carrying equipment, a standard system used for attaching gear and equipment to military and tactical packs, vests, and other load-bearing equipment. MOLLE consists of durable nylon webbing stitched onto the surface of backpacks, vests, and other gear, forming rows of loops. Accessories and pouches equipped with MOLLE-compatible straps can be threaded through these loops, allowing for secure attachment. This system enables the customization and modular arrangement of equipment based on the specific needs of the user, allowing for efficient access and distribution of weight. MOLLE attachments are widely used by military personnel, law enforcement, and outdoor enthusiasts for their flexibility and adaptability in organizing and carrying gear and supplies.

In certain circumstances, it may be prudent to opt for a more inconspicuous pack that does not exude a tactical appearance.

One area may require wearing a camo jacket or the presence of a tactical backpack, seamlessly blending into the fabric of the surroundings, while an inconspicuous tracksuit could be entirely out of place in that context. However, it is essential to acknowledge that the notion of being a "gray man" is not a one-size-fits-all concept; it is highly contextual and dependent on the specific environment in which you find yourself. It is imperative to assess the unique dynamics of each setting and tailor your approach accordingly. The ultimate goal is to render yourself as unremarkable as possible, avoiding attracting undue attention that could potentially compromise your safety.

It is also important to acknowledge that the perception of being an easy target may transcend appearances. Even if your attire or choice of backpack is inconspicuous, if you are perceived as vulnerable or lacking in awareness, predatory individuals may still deem you as a potential target. Therefore, it is paramount to cultivate a holistic approach to personal safety that encompasses both physical appearance and mental preparedness. Strive to project an air of confidence, maintain vigilant situational awareness, and exhibit assertive body language that deters potential threats.

While the "gray man" theory provides invaluable guidance, it is crucial to recognize that adaptability and contextuality are key. Each environment presents its unique challenges and demands a nuanced approach. By continuously assessing your surroundings and adapting your appearance and behavior accordingly, you enhance your chances of remaining unnoticed and ensuring your well-being.

Personal Protection

Personal protection is critical. It keeps you from being a victim. I learned early on, after being targeted by a group of bullies, that I was not able to stand up for myself physically. I was not the 6′3″, 245-pound linebacker I am today. Back in those days, I was a tall, skinny kid. I was not a rich kid, so my stepdad taught me boxing, and I took to wrestling in school. These were great self-defense disciplines, but these styles had fighting rules. So, as I could not afford martial arts classes, when my friends returned from their various courses, whether tae kwon do, judo, aikido, Kenpō, or whatever, I had them teach me all they learned.

Focusing on my survival during childhood gave me a lot of self-confidence, built muscle, and gave me, no pun intended, a fighting chance. My folks were divorced when I was young, and I was quite emotional as a child. The other children in my neighborhood and school picked up on that, which made me a target for bullies. This made me realize quickly I was going to need to rely on myself and truly only count on me. No one had my back. I was made fun of because I was poor, because I had patches on my hand-me-down pants and had to go through the special aid lunch line.

So, I learned to play every sport I could and worked hard to get just good enough to not get picked last. That helped me physically and mentally get stronger. Learning self-defense disciplines in all areas gave me great confidence to finally stand up for myself and not be a target anymore. My childhood made me tough both mentally and physically. I developed a stronger mindset and a no-surrender attitude that carried over into the rest of my life.

You may be a person who is against firearms, and that is fine, but that does not mean the other guy is too. I am all about responsible and safe firearms ownership. Firearms safety was ingrained in me as a small boy from my dad and is still my way now. I am in the camp that firearms do not kill people; people kill people. I also believe that if evil is in one's heart and they are hell-bent on causing harm, they will find a way, whether using a gun, knife, bat, car, etc.

If you find yourself caught in a situation of civil unrest where violence escalates and gunfire erupts, it's crucial to prioritize your safety immediately. Being pinned down in such a volatile environment can be terrifying and dangerous. In such scenarios, seeking immediate cover to protect yourself from bullets and flying debris is vital. Look for solid barriers like concrete walls, metal objects, or even underground spaces that can offer some level of protection. Staying calm and assessing your surroundings for possible escape routes or safer areas to relocate to is essential. Additionally, it's important to avoid drawing attention to yourself, moving cautiously and using the chaos as a cover to find a way out of the danger zone. Keeping a low profile and avoiding confrontation can be key strategies in navigating through areas of civil unrest where shooting is occurring. Remember, the primary goal is to distance yourself from the threat and find a safe haven until the situation stabilizes or help arrives.

Technology has come a long way in recent years, and there are great alternatives to carrying full body armor and plate setup if you should happen to need that. They make backpacks with armor inside that can be opened and worn as body armor, protecting the front and back of your body. If you are already carrying a bag, why not use one that can save you if bullets start flying?

What if your bug-out bag is in your vehicle, and as 1 mentioned earlier, you cannot carry a lot of EDC gear? That is where specific gear can be a lifesaver. A company called Wazoo Survival Gear created a belt called the "Cache Belt" and a hat called the "Cache Cap." These products have a ton of hidden pockets where you can easily store gear, such as cash, a small compass, escape and evasion gear, a lockpick set, a razor blade or knife, and so much more, all within the confines of your belt and hat. These are pretty genius products, if you ask me. Gear like this gives you a fighting chance to get through bad situations.

Personal protection encompasses a multifaceted approach that combines physical prowess, mental preparedness, and the utilization of appropriate gear. Equipping ourselves with the necessary skills and tools not only enhances our ability to ward off potential threats but also instills a sense of empowerment and peace of mind. By arming ourselves with a diverse range of self-defense techniques and staying abreast of emerging technologies, we can navigate the complexities of an unpredictable world with confidence and resilience.

Vehicle-Specific Kits

The significance of my vehicle as a rolling survival kit has been ingrained in me for as long as I can remember. It all began when I was just seventeen years old, a newly minted driver venturing into the vast world with my very first car. The trunk of that vehicle became a treasure trove of possibilities, a space where I could store essential items that could prove invaluable during emergencies. I meticulously filled it with a range of provisions, including water jugs, blankets, candles, tools, and even kitty litter for the harsh winter months; it would serve to give me traction if I ever found myself stuck in the snow. It became abundantly clear that a well-equipped vehicle could make the difference between survival and dire circumstances.

Picture this: you've successfully reached your vehicle, the sanctuary that holds your salvation in this challenging moment. The question arises, "What lies within the confines of your trunk?" Your vehicle now transforms into a large "Get You Home Bag," and the contents it houses become paramount. With the addition of your "Get to Your Car Bag" setup, your capabilities for survival and navigation significantly increase. The fusion of these two elements forms your ultimate "Get You Home Bag." The underlying principle is to ensure that your vehicle is adequately prepared to support and facilitate your journey back to safety.

So, what should you consider including in your car to bolster your chances of a successful homeward journey? Let's explore a list of essential items and factors to consider:

Vehicle Gear List

- Vehicle (no matter your ride, it needs to be in good working order, serviced, and topped off on all fluids)
- Paper maps (road and topographic)
- Additional communication is optional, like a CB or ham radio or satellite phone
- Spare tire with working jack and tire iron
- Small tool bag with essential tools in it and flashlight with extra batteries
- Road flares (excellent fire starters and signaling devices)
- Extra fuel can, oil, and other fluids
- Small shovel
- Tow straps and chains
- Extra fresh water, buckets of premade freeze-dried food, or vacuum-sealed foods, such as rice, pasta, etc. If you store foods like pasta and rice, be sure you have a way to boil water.
- Large tarp, extra rope, cordage, or paracord, and sleeping bag and or blankets
- Full "bug-out bag" in case your vehicle breaks down or you must bail out of your car due to the situation
- Winter kit if in a snowy area, like tire snow chains, ice melt, cat litter, snow shovel, candles, winter clothing (hats, gloves, boots, etc.)
- Faraday bag to store your electronics. (Faraday bags, or EMP bags, block ionizing radiation from a high-altitude EMP. You can keep a spare engine control unit and an OBD scanner to program it with if you have the correct type of vehicle that does not rely on anything more than that electronically to be able to run.)

Your vehicle takes center stage as the primary mode of transportation that will navigate you safely back home. It is imperative to ensure that your vehicle remains in optimal working condition, as its reliability is essential. Equally crucial is the inclusion of essential items within your vehicle that will fortify its functionality and enhance your chances of reaching your destination unscathed.

As your mobile sanctuary, your vehicle offers a multitude of advantages that can significantly impact your survival. First, it provides protection against the elements, shielding you from harsh weather conditions and providing a refuge of relative comfort. Second, it enables you to conserve energy, as traversing long distances on foot can be physically demanding and exhausting. Your vehicle serves as a reliable means of covering substantial ground swiftly and efficiently. Last, it has the capacity to carry an abundance of supplies, ensuring that you have the necessary resources at your disposal throughout your journey.

The items that you have thoughtfully brought along now assume an integral role within your survival "Get You Home Bag." These provisions serve as your lifeline, acting as a safety net that augments your chances of returning home safely and in one piece. If your vehicle encounters mechanical issues or unforeseen circumstances that necessitate your departure from the car, your bug-out bag assumes an even greater significance.

The bug-out bag is a critical component of your survival arsenal, functioning as a contingency plan in case you must abandon your vehicle and proceed on foot. Stocked with essential supplies tailored to sustain you during an extended journey, this well-equipped bag encompasses a diverse range of items, including food, water, shelter, clothing, communication devices, tools, and other necessities designed to support your survival and ensure your well-being.

While your vehicle provides invaluable advantages, it is essential to acknowledge that it may not be infallible. Mechanical failures or circumstances beyond your control may force you to rely solely on your bug-out bag and your physical capabilities. Therefore, it is imperative to allocate the necessary time and attention to assembling a comprehensive bug-out bag that aligns with your unique needs and circumstances.

I remember once I was in my truck adventuring way off the beaten path. I was heading for an outing for several days to a remote wilderness area in the mountains. A friend had told me about a nice spot with a stream that had huge trout in it. I got off the road onto the firebreak trails and started winding my way in across some rugged roads.

It was an amazing journey with magical views as I went through the mountains. Once I got about seventy-five miles in, I found the spot I was told about and set up camp, then got a fishing line in the water. The first couple of days were great, and then the clouds started coming in. The weather forecast wasn't calling for severe weather, but then again, Mother Nature can be unpredictable.

It started storming like crazy a few hours later with extremely high winds. It got really bad fast. Trees were starting to come down, and water was starting to rush off the sides of the mountains. I decided to wait it out, but it kept going. It went on all night and into the next morning. I decided that I had had enough, and it was time to go.

There was only one trail into the area where I was, so I only had one way to get back out. I started up the mountain trail and it was hairy even for an experienced off-roader like me. The trail was in very slick condition and trees had fallen onto the road. I was able to make it past several of those trees, but my truck started sliding due to the slick, wet, muddy conditions. I tried hard to maintain control but soon found myself heading straight for a massive tree that blocked the road, and as I turned slightly to avoid hitting it head-on, my truck skidded off the road, blowing out a tire and high centering the truck on some rocks. (High centering is when your vehicle frame gets stuck on top of rocks or a ledge and your tires are no longer touching the ground.)

I tried for a while in four-wheel drive, placing logs and debris under the tires in an attempt to self-rescue, but it was no use. The hard lesson I learned was that not having a winch in a situation like this sucked. But these are the lessons that I have learned in life that are most impactful, and ones you don't repeat.

Realizing I was way out in the middle of nowhere without any park rangers in this wilderness area, and no one expecting me for another four days, I was in a pickle. I had enough supplies to camp for a while, but what if no one came by to help me? And the trail I was on wasn't one that was well travelled. So, I decided to grab my Go Bag and hike out to either find someone to help or give me a ride or walk to the end of the trail back to civilization.

Thankfully the storm had slowed down to a slight drizzle. I grabbed my bug-out bag, my knife, and my pistol, and off I went. My bug-out bag had everything I needed to survive and take care of my needs. I was in good shape, and for me hiking was easy since I was training often with my bag on me. I had all I needed in the bag to set up camp each night, resupply fresh water, cook at least one hot meal a day, and make coffee.

I trekked across the rugged mountain terrain for about four days, until I got to the main firebreak that was on the map. I started down that trail and about three hours later a wildfire truck pulled up. I explained to them my situation and they offered to help. I jumped in and showed them on the map roughly where I had left my truck.

They knew the area and said there were a lot of mudslides there. Off we went, and they were rather impressed at my calmness and that I had been trekking and camping along the way for four days. Seems I covered some forty-seven miles. They got me back to my truck, now partially covered by thick mud. They broke out chain saws and made fast work of the massive tree covering the trail road. Then they used their winch to pull my truck out. I loaded up, thanked them, and kissed the winch. This is why you should always keep a bug-out bag with you at all times, and a winch on your vehicle.

Your vehicle assumes a pivotal role in your survival journey, acting as your primary mode of transportation and offering an array of advantages that enhance your chances of reaching your destination safely. It becomes your mobile shelter, energy-conserving vehicle, and carrier of essential supplies.

However, the bug-out bag stands as your dependable backup plan, ready to support you should the need arise to abandon your vehicle. By prioritizing the maintenance of your vehicle, equipping it with vital resources, and preparing a well-stocked bug-out bag, you establish a robust framework for a successful journey home, ensuring your safety and resilience in the face of adversity.

"Bug-out" or "Get Home" Bags

You may not be like me, a guy who can just head out to the wilderness with a knife and survive; however, do not get me wrong, I like my comfort items too. The argument of what goes in the perfect bug-out bag may never be settled, but for me, it's all about your needs, must-haves, budget, situation, and what I call plain old "skullcrushing sense." Which is just like common sense but with attitude. Below you will find a suggested list of things to consider in *your* bug-out bag setup:

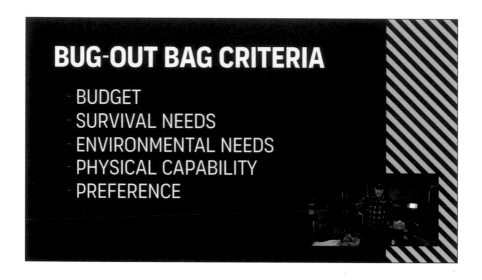

BUG-OUT BAG CRITERIA
- BUDGET
- SURVIVAL NEEDS
- ENVIRONMENTAL NEEDS
- PHYSICAL CAPABILITY
- PREFERENCE

My Recommended Bug-Out Bag Gear List

These are some of the items I recommend, but do not focus on the exact brands of each product (though I will mention some for referencing). Focus on which needs each item is fulfilling for you. When I use the term bug-out bag, I'm also referring to a get-home bag.

Backpacks
- 5.11 COVRT18 backpack
- 5.11 RUSH 12 2.0, RUSH 24, or RUSH 72 backpack

- Mystery Ranch backpacks
- CamelBak water bladder for the inside of your pack

Fire

- Überleben ferrocerium rod
- Exotac fire sleeve
- UCO stormproof matches
- Purefire tactical magnesium fire starter
- Live Fire gear tin
- Fatwood shavings
- Beeswax candles

Shelter

- Supplemental shelter kit—Shelter BOSS kit
- Mil-Tec poncho (two can make a shelter)
- 100 percent virgin wool blanket(s)
- Waterproof tarp
- Snugpak Stasha G2 Shelter
- Snugpak SF Bivvi
- Mil-Tec Hollowfibre Mummy sleeping bag
- Poncho liner, aka the "woobie"
- Paracord (100 feet)
- #36 bank line (twisted, tarred nylon cordage)

Water

- Grayl GeoPress
- Sawyer Mini
- Water purification tablets
- Single-wall stainless steel container
- Cotton shemagh

Food

- SOS emergency rations
- Homemade pemmican
- PowerBars
- Clif Bars

First Aid

- Quality individual first aid kit (IFAK) (trauma kit)
- Extra Gen. 7 C.A.T. tourniquet
- Basic first aid kit

(Continued on next page)

Navigation
- Suunto compass
- Compass cards
- Pace beads
- Local topographical maps mytopo.com 1:50 scale
- Waterproof notebook and pencil
- Handheld GPS (not your phone!)

Communications
- Satellite phone
- CB radio
- Ham radios
- Walkie-talkies

Tools
- Mountain Predator knife
- TOPS SXB
- Silky Saw
- Morakniv Garberg knife with leather sheath
- Viking whetstone sharpening necklace

Supplemental items
- Wool socks (a couple of pairs) and an extra T-shirt
- Hygiene kit
- Insect repellent or netting
- Any required medication
- Handheld GPS units such as Garmin 64ST or Garmin watch
- Solar-powered device chargers

Winter and other supplemental gear
- Extra 100 percent virgin wool blanket
- Winter boots, hats, gloves
- Polypropylene tops and bottom
- Baklava
- Ice-fishing sled (to help carry your pack and supplemental gear if necessary)

What about prescription medication? Do you have enough with you to last for a few days? What about a tourniquet? If you carry a knife or a firearm, you should also carry a tourniquet, such as the Gen. 7 C.A.T. tourniquet from North American Rescue. If you have the power to take a life, you should also have the power to save a life. Another great item to have in your vehicle is a set of moleskin bandages. Blisters can slow you down quickly if you must walk long distances, and moleskin bandages are a lifesaver.

Depending on the size of your pack, the time of year, and supplemental gear you may need, you may be unable to fit all your gear in one bag. Some opt to keep extra equipment in the vehicle and use an ice-fishing sled to pull supplemental gear in the winter.

Do you live in a more urban area? Maybe you need other supplemental items like wire cutters or a screwdriver. If you have encountered a situation where you might need to cut some wires or even hotwire a vehicle, a quality multi-tool is a must-have item. Another item I like to carry is a Silcox key. That particular type of key can turn on commercial water spigots, so you can fill up your stainless steel container or water bottle to keep yourself hydrated while you are on the move.

Getting from Your Vehicle to Your Home

Now that you have reached point B, which is your vehicle, it's time to focus on getting to point C, your home, where you plan to hunker down and "bug in." Before starting your journey, it is essential to conduct a quick assessment of your vehicle's condition. Check that there are no signs of tampering or unauthorized access. Take a moment to inspect the tires, ensuring they are properly inflated and free from damage. Additionally, check under the hood to see if everything appears intact and that no fuel has been siphoned from your vehicle.

However, before entering your vehicle, it is crucial to exercise situational awareness and remain vigilant. Scan your surroundings and make sure there are no potential threats lurking nearby. Be cautious of anyone who may be loitering or exhibiting suspicious behavior, and take a moment to assess the area as you approach your vehicle.

Once you have confirmed the immediate vicinity is secure, it's time to conduct an internal check of your vehicle. Look through the windows and into the back seat to make sure no one is hiding inside, waiting to ambush you.

With the vehicle cleared and deemed safe, it's time to proceed to your primary location as swiftly as possible. Keep in mind that time may be of the essence, so exercise caution but also maintain a sense of urgency. Prioritize a direct and secure route to your home, utilizing familiar roads and avoiding potential areas of unrest or congestion.

As you navigate toward your destination, remain vigilant and aware of your surroundings. Monitor radio updates or reliable sources of information to stay informed about any potential hazards or changing circumstances along your route. Adjust your course if necessary to avoid any high-risk areas.

Once you arrive at your home, be prepared to quickly secure your perimeter and ensure its integrity. Lock all entry points, reinforce doors and windows if necessary, and establish a sense of security within your immediate surroundings. Remember, maintaining a strong sense of situational awareness remains paramount even within the confines of your home.

In conclusion, transitioning from point B (your vehicle) to point C (your home) requires careful consideration and the application of situational awareness. By conducting a thorough assessment of your vehicle, remaining vigilant during the approach, and practicing caution throughout your journey, you can minimize potential risks and increase your chances of safely reaching your bug-in location. Remember, adaptability and swift decision-making are key as you navigate the uncertain terrain, aiming to secure your ultimate sanctuary: your home.

Setting Up and Maintaining Caches

What happens if you break down on your way home in your vehicle and must start moving on foot? As part of your PACE plan, it is a good idea to set up multiple cache points halfway between where your work is or where you start and your home. At your predetermined cache spots is where you might keep extra gear, such as extra ammunition and magazines, extra food, fuel, water, and first aid supplies. The supplies in your cache locations are only there if you need to resupply or become separated from your main bug-out bag.

Now that you are in your vehicle and heading to your domicile with a backup plan, all is well, right? Wrong; it seems the riot has cut off your primary route and your alternate. Thankfully, you were planning and had a contingency plan that takes you to a "hold up" spot at one of several cache sites you planned for and have in place. So, what exactly is a cache site?

A cache site is a location you can reach either by vehicle or on foot and that is off the beaten path so as not to draw attention. This spot should be hidden but easy for you to find by day or night. It should be marked so that if anyone sees it, it does not cause them to investigate but allows them to help you find it. Marking might involve doing something like removing bark in the shape of a square and maybe having more than one on the tree. It means something to you but not the unsuspecting passerby. You know that ten paces from this spot in a certain direction, you have a buried cache waiting for you. Some folks may stack rocks on top of each other. I have even used spray paint graffiti in more urban settings. It should provide some cover from the eyesight of others and protection from the elements and be easily defendable. You can mark your cache location in some way to quickly find it, but I generally like to make a small strip map of each cache site and pace the buried site off from a known point, like a recognizable tree covertly marked. When marking a cache location on a map or a GPS unit, write down your central location, such as a tree or structure. Once your main point is marked, pace off the exact location of your cache so that if someone gets a hold of your marked area, only you would know the precise location of the supply. A good hidden cache can have folks who might have decided that the area you chose would make a good campsite for the night, setting up right on top of it and not even know they're sitting on a treasure chest.

What I mean by "pace off" is that if you choose a specific tree or other easily identifiable landmark, walk fifty paces away from that landmark in one direction, and then change directions and walk another fifty paces. I like digging a hole and burying my cache in a waterproof Pelican case or even heavy-duty PVC tubing with an end that can be screwed on and off. Once in the ground, you can cover the cache supplies with an old tarp or some wood, throw the dirt right over it, and camouflage the area, and you are good to go.

You will also have already hidden caches there in some fashion. Whether you bury your supplies or hide them by camouflage, you need to ensure they cannot be found and stolen because you want them there for you when you need them. They will act to support you without dipping into your vehicle setup or bug-out bag, as well as resupply what you used. There are many ways to set them up. The area where you place your supplies must have enough space to hide them, or you need to dig a big enough hole to bury them. You can use a natural brush to hide them by camouflage. Over time, vegetation dies and turns brown, so I recommend using military camo netting or an old canvas tarp that you can spray-paint with colors to match the area.

Here is an example: My main point is a large oak tree that is easily recognizable, which is the only location I list on my map or GPS unit. Once I am at that point, I would walk 50–100 paces east or west, then walk 50–100 paces north or south, where I would place my cache in the ground. If I am pacing out fifty feet north and then fifty feet east, I would use that same pacing for all my cache locations to not forget the pattern. I also would stash a D-handle shovel somewhere, so you are not stuck using your hands to get your cache out of the ground. You must also plan for the wintertime if the ground freezes in your area. Maybe some of your cache locations are abandoned structures and not buried.

Lastly, I have known folks to just be obvious about it and drop a metal storage container, dumpster, locker, container, or shed at a spot and throw a lock and chains on it. I even knew a guy who used a porta-potty. Now, the cache supplies themselves can be packaged in many ways. I use various methods to do this, and here are a few suggestions. I love old military canvas duffel bags. I usually stuff the items in heavy-duty leaf trash bags (this is an added layer of protection, waterproofing, and preservation) and then tape them closed with duct tape before putting them in the duffel bag.

Duffel bags are generally suitable for almost any items, like extra batteries, gear, food, etc. I also like using footlockers with a lock on them separately and packaging the supplies for additional protection. Plastic heavy-duty tote boxes work well. You place your supplies inside them, again individually packaged for safety, and seal the totes with duct tape. Then for the third layer of protection, put the totes in heavy-duty leaf trash bags before you are done. All these steps help protect your supplies from the elements and wildlife.

For fuel, I use plastic five-gallon containers. For water, I prefer five-gallon plastic jugs, gallon milk jugs or two-liter plastic bottles, or collapsible water jugs. I will even store dry-cut firewood in plastic trash bags, so it is ready to go with a few bags of tinder, kindling, and even some fire starters. Now is not the time to go bushcrafty. Below is a list of my recommended cache site items.

Recommended Cache Site Gear

- Extra fuel cans
- Extra water cans
- Kindling and fire-starting gear
- Food
- Batteries
- Extra survival gear and supplies
- Tent
- Clothes
- Ammo
- Extra first aid gear

A hold-up site with a cache will give you a place to refit, rest, and adjust your plans. You should be able to stay there for a few hours or up to a few days. I usually try to only plan for seventy-two hours max and then get mobile or head to the next hold-up cache site if I cannot get home. All these things we have discussed here are things you need to be thinking about and planning, as your safety and success in getting back home depend on it. Having your home ready for bug-in does you no good if you cannot even get there.

You Have Made It Home; Now What?

I wish I could tell you the exact number of times in my life I had natural disasters strike, and I was so glad I was prepared. Planning for an emergency gave me the foundation to prepare for that survival scenario where I had to bug in. It's all about keeping you and your loved ones safe, prepared, and alive.

We saw this happen during the COVID-19 pandemic, and many folks were not adequately prepared. Many people quickly ran out of supplies, food, medical needs, and other things. Store shelves emptied quickly. Factories and distribution centers shut down. Transport by trucks, rail, and air came to a halt. So many people in the world were left wondering how they got to this point.

The answer is straightforward: without planning. People may say well, that was a once-in-a-lifetime event. Well, was it? Never make the mistake of assuming that a disaster or emergency will not come knocking on your door when it comes to your and your loved ones' survival. A myriad of things can happen and will happen, and it is just a matter of when. So, the time is now; that's when planning for these things matters most. The next pandemic, hurricane, earthquake, civil unrest, wildfire, war, etc., could be just around the corner. Do not be caught with your pants down and wondering why this happened. Be the solution to your problem by acting. You do not need to be a millionaire to prepare; there are many budget-friendly options to fit all economic situations.

So, the first of many things you need to do is assess where you are in your preparedness. Start a list by category to get that survival preparedness laundry list going and fill it up. It is a critical step in the process and will help keep you on track, even sane, and clarify your needs. I am old school, so I always grab a sheet of paper, a pencil, and a clipboard. Electronics are great, but this

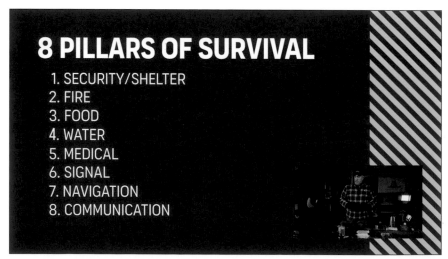

8 PILLARS OF SURVIVAL
1. SECURITY/SHELTER
2. FIRE
3. FOOD
4. WATER
5. MEDICAL
6. SIGNAL
7. NAVIGATION
8. COMMUNICATION

is one thing you need to see every day and often, as a staunch reminder of what you've got but more so what you still need. Here is a sample list, and everyone's list will be different. In later chapters, I will get into specific details on each category shown on my home preparedness list.

Home Preparedness List

Shelter & Tools

- Radio
- Extra blankets or sleeping bags
- Shelving for storing your gear
- Backup generator
- Extension cords
- Solar chargers
- Tent or canvas tarps
- Exterior solar panels with batteries inside
- Tools for building structures, repairs, and recovery

Navigation

- Extra fuel for generator and vehicles
- Flashlights
- Extra batteries
- Head lamps
- Compass
- Candles
- Road maps and topographical maps

Water

- Several five-gallon water jugs (the five-gallon LifeSaver Jerrycan purifies water and is a great choice)
- Several water filter systems like Sawyer Mini or MSR backpack pumps
- Individual water bottles (two for each person). I recommend single-wall stainless steel ones so that if you have to purify water as a backup, you can boil water in them.

(Continued on next page)

- A filter system, such as the Grayl GeoPress, a few extra filters for the GeoPress, and a single-wall stainless steel container
- A few fifty-five-gallon drums that can be stored in your basement or garage
- A series of fifty-five-gallon drums that can be connected to your roof's gutter system. This will depend on the exact type of rain catch system you're going to use, and how many downspouts you have at your property. I usually like to have one drum at every gutter pipe coming off the roof of the home and garage to maximize water gathering. The water can be used for drinking, hygiene, animals, and watering crops and plants. I like to set up leaf catch screens or as you have seen on TV the "leaf gutter" systems to keep leaves, sticks, and other particles out of your water. I also place a screen catchment at the top on each drum's entry point as a backup. Remember they need to be cleared out regularly. If it's not during an emergency and you're collecting rainwater regularly, be sure to check if there are any limitations on rainwater collection in your state. Some states that are prone to droughts, such as California, have regulations on rainwater collection.
- Water purification tablets
- Plain bleach with no additives or color-safe features

Food
- Extra nonperishable foods and canned goods
- Coolers
- Cases of dehydrated or freeze-dried meals
- MREs
- Camp meals
- Jerky and dehydrated fruits
- Nuts or trail mix
- Energy meal bars
- Pots and utensils

Fire and Cooking
- BBQ grill
- Camp stove with extra fuel tanks
- Extra propane
- Fireplace
- Plenty of firewood
- Wood-burning stoves/electric or propane heaters
- Firepits

Security
- Alarm system
- Security cameras
- Fencing/gates
- Locks
- Anti-pick door locks
- Dead bolts
- Security lights
- A safe for your valuables
- Firearms
- Knives
- Alternate defense weapons, such as expandable batons, a baseball bat, or other impact weapons
- Extra ammo
- Mace or pepper spray
- Taser
- Home and auto 3M anti-smash security glass film
- I often have several of these items hidden in each room all over the house so they are there when I need them.

Medical
- First aid kit
- Prescription meds
- Pain relievers
- Trauma kits w/extra tourniquets
- Extra batteries
- Saline and an IV kit
- Suture kit

Survival Matrix

I fully understand how difficult it can be when you run into tough times. I have been there myself and had to deal with things like inflation, loss of a job, and other financial responsibilities. It can make preparing even more challenging than when you are not under stress already. So, you need to look at what you have on hand and what you can afford in terms of what you need, and sometimes think outside the box for solutions. That is a must.

While this is just a sample, you get the point; you should start by listing everything you need on the list, then make another couple of columns right next to it with one saying maybe "On Hand" or "Yes" and the other column saying "Need" or "No" and make a check as to where you are. Next, make a fourth column with "Quantity," which is extremely important to ensure that you have enough of each item. As you consume goods, the list is updated. You should also make a fifth column stating a "Par," a number you always want to be as close to as possible for your family's needs, and then a column each for "Cost" and "Notes."

This type of survival matrix will help you see the bigger picture of where you at in your planning. Now breathe. I know it is a lot, and you are probably shocked right now at how far behind you are and in need. That is okay. You have done the hard part, which is a start, so get after the immediate needs and start filling in where you can immediately based on your situation and budget. You may highlight or put a little star next to the most important things. You must do what you can to knock out the list, fill shelves, install items, etc. Get moving!

CATEGORY ITEMS	ITEMS ON HAND	EST. COST OF ITEMS	ADDITIONAL TRAINING, CERT., & PRACTICE	NOTES
MINDSET & SKILLS				
Current survival skill level (to include hunting, trapping, & fishing skills)				
Current self defense level (including armed and unarmed)				
Current situational awareness & attention to details skills				
Reference material library (electronic, books, magazines, & notes)				
GETTING TO MY VEHICLE FROM WORK/ SCHOOL/OTHER LOCATION				
Defense items				
Water bottle				
Small survival pack				
Tools/pocket knife				
GETTING HOME ONCE AT MY VEHICLE				
Vehicle in good mechanical order (tires, fluids, engine, etc)				
Defense items				
Additional seasonal items for region and weather (winter kit)				
Spare tire with jack				
Tool bag w/ tools				
Shovel				
Additional water				
Blankets (preferably wool)				
Bug-out bag, fully loaded (see list on p. 24)				
Additional fuel/oil/washer fluids				

(Continued on next page)

CATEGORY ITEMS	ITEMS ON HAND	EST. COST OF ITEMS	ADDITIONAL TRAINING, CERT., & PRACTICE	NOTES
Paper maps for routes				
Bicycle w/ additional spare parts and tire tubes				
Communication—cell, walkie talkie, cb, ham radio, satellite phone, portable radio for info				
BUG-OUT BAG ITEMS (BASIC SUGGESTIONS, NOT SPECIFIC ITEMS)				
Bug-out bag—comfortable pack that can carry 3 to 5 days of needs				
Water bottles—1 w/ filter & 1 steel canteen				
Water filters, water purification tabs, steel cup or small pot to boil				
Fire starting items—lighters, magnesium fire starter, etc				
Survival tools (fixed blade survival knife, axe, machete, saw, etc)				
Paracord				
Shelter—either small tent or tarp				
Food—dehydrated meals or MREs, or other non-perishables like jerky				
Cooking system and pot				
Hunting and fishing items—fishing kit, snare wire, slingshot, bow, etc				
Sleeping system—sleeping bag or bedroll				
Waterproof windbreaker or raincoat				
Work gloves and eye protection				
Additional change of clothes and 3 pairs of good socks w/ good footgear				

CATEGORY ITEMS	ITEMS ON HAND	EST. COST OF ITEMS	ADDITIONAL TRAINING, CERT., & PRACTICE	NOTES
Hygiene items				
Medicines and prescription meds				
First aid kit				
Additional helpful survival items (cotton bandana, candles, etc)				
Headlamp, flashlight, compass				
Communication—cell, walkie talkie, CB, ham, portable radio for info				
CACHE STOP POINTS (NEED THEM SET UP ON ALL ROUTES HOME)				
Additional water (5-gallon jugs)				
Additional fuel (5-gallon cans)				
Additional food				
Additional gear and equipment				
Tarp and camoflague to hide cache & covert marking system				

Some budget-friendly things you can do, for example, if you cannot buy a bunch of five-gallon camp water containers, is start saving milk jugs and two-liter plastic bottles. Rinse them, fill them with water, and then use a permanent marker to write the current date. This way, you will know how old they are. I love permanent markers, and writing dates on items where they are prominent and visible helps you out.

I mark the expiration dates on all food items, so in my food rotation, I consume stuff that expires before other things. I only dip into long-shelf-life supplies if I have no other options. It's this type of thinking that helps you get ahead of the curve. I always look for grocery store sales, and when I see canned food deals, I buy up as much as I can and store it. You can even plan to purchase three survival-planning items each time you go to the store during your regular grocery shopping time. Before you know it, your shelves are filling up fast.

I even visit those great and abundant Dollar Stores. You will be surprised by how affordable the items are and how many quality items you can get in large amounts without breaking the bank. You can knock down that list fast, even if you are on a strict budget. It is called thinking outside the box and making it happen, as your survival depends on it. These are just a few examples to get your brain churning.

Now, when it comes to storage, that also depends on your domicile situation. Somebody in a rural area, say on a farm, may have several outbuildings and designate one for their survival storage area. Suburban types may have a basement or garage, which can apply to a townhome. Things get trickier for urbanites, but being a professional hoarder, I can tell you that every nook and cranny counts and can be used.

I usually suggest that those in apartment situations consider getting an apartment for what they need in terms of bedrooms plus one. This way, you have sleep spaces for everyone and one extra room, usually at least a 10' × 10' size, to set up shelving and make it a survival supply storage area. Don't forget about laundry rooms, utility closets, attics, crawl spaces, and sheds for additional space. I recommend good sturdy shelves. You can buy some plastic shelving of different types and sturdiness, get some metal racks, or build wooden ones. Even wall lockers can work and give you the ability to lock them up for added security. I also suggest you categorize your shelf or storage areas by type, like water, food, medical, etc.

All these tips and things should now have your mind immersed in the planning and stocking phase of bugging in. They say an ounce of prevention is worth a pound of cure, so that holds here, and I like to say, "good planning prevents pain" in that you have taken care of your needs and then some, are fully stocked, and are now ready for what may come . . . and it will come!

CHAPTER 3

SELF-DEFENSE AND WEAPONS

Focusing on self-defense, it's crucial to be prepared for any situation that might arise, whether you're at home, at work, or out in public. This means not only having the right tools at your disposal, such as a firearm, pepper spray, or even a flashlight that can also be used as an impact weapon, but also acquiring the knowledge and skills to use them effectively. Training in self-defense techniques can significantly enhance your ability to protect yourself and others from harm. It's about being aware of your surroundings, understanding the dynamics of a threatening situation, and knowing how to respond swiftly and decisively. By prioritizing self-defense, you equip yourself with the confidence and capabilities needed to navigate potentially dangerous situations with greater assurance and control.

You have made it home and mentally, you should start feeling calmer and in control now. You got where you needed to be, and you should be proud of that. The great thing about your home is that it is your shelter; it is your castle. It gives you a sense of

safety and security whether natural disasters are coming, or you are preparing to bug in for the long haul due to civil unrest or another large-scale catastrophe that has struck your city or town, your entire state, or even the country.

The best way to make sure that you are mentally ready to go, can stay calm, and can keep the stressors out of your life is to use the PACE plan you have put together to allow you to be ready to go no matter what the situation is. You have all your gear and supplies and have been practicing what to do in any scenario. You have put in the time to train with your family to ensure that everyone is on the same page regarding preparedness and enacting your plan.

Firearms

Your home is your castle, and all castles need to be defended. Security is paramount if someone is trying to break in to cause you harm or steal your supplies, so you will need the right equipment to protect your castle. All kinds of options are available, from the obvious to the not-so-obvious. Well, let us start with the obvious.

First off, I would like to talk about firearms. If you are not big into weapons, this may not be an option. I respect your thoughts, but this is the highest escalation. When someone comes to harm you or your family, if they have firearms and you do not have anything to match that kind of threat level, then you have already taken yourself out of the fight if they make it inside your home, and you must defend yourself. The old adage, "Don't bring a knife to a gunfight!" rings so true here. I remember watching an episode of *Doomsday Preppers* one time and experts grade the participants on how they have set up for "SHTF" situations and you see all kinds of stuff. In this particular episode, these folks in New England had gathered together and built an amazing community. They had it all: there were lots of families that supported each other in the community, everyone had a specialty skill they had mastered, and most folks had lots of crossover skills. They had a doctor, a nurse, a dentist, a butcher, many skilled traders, farmers, etc. They all supported each other, traded goods and services, had a leadership panel to handle community issues. They had food, water systems, stockpiles of supplies, the works, except one thing: security. They did not believe in and did not allow firearms into their community. At the end they were very offended when they received high grades across the board but flatlined when it came to security, and that drastically crushed the final score tally in preparedness. They were steadfast in their belief that they would never change that one aspect in their plan. I respect everyone's rights and choices, but thought, well, what if a large group of men showed up armed? Say like the group in the movie *The Postman* where they went from settlement to settlement strong-arming the folks to take all their goods and basically enslave them because they didn't have the means or will to fight back. I for one would never want to be in this situation myself. I remember the rite of passage as a boy to crossing over into manhood was getting to go on that first hunting trip. Attending the hunters' firearms safety class, learning the basics of shooting starting with a BB gun, then a .22 Henry rifle, and up to my daddy's 308, and even my grand-dad's shotgun. All this carried over into the military with me and ever since I have regularly trained with my firearms to always be ready and prepared. Not to be ready to do violence and evil, but to be ready when evil comes knocking on my door. I believe that a firearm in the right capable hands can save lives and save the day. Evil is going to find a way to do evil whether or not they have a gun. History has shown that evil folks will grab a machete, a knife, use a car, explosives, whatever they have at hand.

My point is, most folks who don't like or use firearms or are against them for whatever reason, in my opinion, really don't understand them and that makes them fearful of them. My suggestion is that one should at least start by familiarizing themselves with safe use of firearms. Start by taking a hunters' safety class even if you aren't going to hunt, there you will see folks of all walks of life and ages, and this will help your comfort level. Next take a regular firearms safety course; the NRA puts many on. I am a huge advocate that *all* firearms users *must* take this course. Then, take some classes at the range or go to a shooting range, either indoors or outdoors, and ask if they offer one-on-one coaching or classes. At many of these places the professionals there love teaching folks and may not even charge you.

This is where your home defense starts and, of course, once you are comfortable and purchase firearms, regular use and training is a must so that when you need this survival skill, you are ready. Safe and responsible gun ownership is paramount to keeping everyone safe. I would highly suggest getting as much training as possible to learn how to handle firearms properly, and once you are comfortable with a gun, purchase one to keep inside your home for protection. Having the ability to fend off attackers with equal force will at least give you a fighting chance.

In my opinion, an excellent pistol for protection is a Glock 19, a Smith & Wesson M&P 9mm, or a Sig Sauer P320. There are a lot of great guns on the market, and the ones I have mentioned are just a few of the best and most recommended firearms for home defense. You may also find a short-barrel rifle an excellent asset for home protection. They are very functional; some have collapsible stocks that make close-quarters room clearing and combat much more efficient.

Pistols

Many short-barrel rifles are pistols in a short-barrel rifle type of platform. They are much more compact than a standard AR-15 rifle, and moving about the hallways and close-quartered rooms is much easier. Let us not forget the trusty shotgun. Shotguns are excellent home defense weapons as well. I like them because once you start blasting a shotgun down the hallway, if there are folks in there trying to assault you, especially if it is more than one intruder, you may stand a better chance using a shotgun and loading up double-ought buckshot rounds. 00 Buck essentially sends nine large-caliber pellets over 1,300 feet per second. This round is highly effective in stopping intruders.

Rifles

One of my favorite shotguns fires twelve-gauge shells and comes with a ten-round magazine. It is not a pump shotgun, it is a semi-automatic shotgun, so it is much easier to get rounds on target much more quickly. You will want to use a rifle sling with any good rifle or shotgun. There are many benefits to using a sling; the first would be that you do not have to constantly carry your rifle or shotgun when you are not actively engaging a target. It frees up your hands whenever necessary without putting down or dropping your weapon. If you run out of ammunition and want to draw your pistol quickly, you can do so safely with a rifle sling until you find cover and can reload your rifle. A rifle or shotgun sling is like having a holster for your long gun, like your pistol.

I found a great sling made by a company called Warrior Poet Society. Their sling holds your weapon higher and tighter against your body, making movement much more accessible. It also utilizes a bungee sling action, which allows you to have your gun higher and tighter than traditional slings but can still present your weapon to address threats very quickly without having to loosen the sling. It also features a superfast quick disconnect that utilizes rare earth magnets for connections and disconnections. They call it the "Jedi Buckle." It is light-years better than the slings we used in the Army. I wish I'd had one of these back in my military days, because those regular old slings were terrible.

I said it at the beginning of the chapter, but I cannot stress this enough; get as much training as possible for you and your family and keep training as often as possible. Do not spend $1,000 on a firearm and only a few hundred dollars on training. Do the opposite; spend $500–$1,000 on a gun and $5,000 on training. The

training part of this equation is far more critical than having the best firearm money can buy. Now, if money is no object, then sure, buy the best firearm on the market, *and* get the best training money can buy.

Keep training, though, because firearms training is a perishable skill. If you only train a few times and then do not train regularly after that, in an emergency, you will fall back to your worst level of training. When training, once you get to a comfortable level, good instructors will start to introduce stressors into your training to get your heart racing. Introducing stressors is meant to simulate a real-world survival situation. There is no sense in only training at an air-conditioned indoor shooting range with no distractions because, in a real-life situation, this will not be the case.

Some of the best firearms instructors on the planet can be found at sheepdogresponse.com, owned by Green Beret and Special Forces sniper Tim Kennedy. You can also find great training courses at Warrior Poet Society. There are a lot of fantastic instructors and schools out there. I am just giving you a couple of examples of some of the best.

Knives

Of course, a knife is not as effective as a firearm, but it is the next level of lethality, and when you are defending yourself or your loved ones, and people's lives are on the line, it is better than not having a weapon at all. In fact, with proper training, a knife can be one of the deadliest weapons for self-defense, especially in close-quarter combat situations. I have known well-trained soldiers and fighters who are deathly afraid of going up against a knife in a close-quarters case.

Even some of the best fighters on the planet risk getting cut by a knife attacker that possesses any level of skill. Suppose you have never watched videos online that show simulated attacks where a person with a knife attacks a person with a gun. In that case, the attacker can close the distance from twenty feet or less faster than the other person can draw, aim, and shoot their firearm. Watching these drills is an eye-opening experience, and it shows you just how dangerous a knife can be.

I put many folding knives throughout my house, some up high on top of cabinets or appliances, some in kitchen drawers or dressers, and even some under tables, hidden all about in case I am moving around, something happens unexpectedly, and I cannot get to my safe to retrieve my firearm. After all, most of us will not always be walking around our houses with a shoulder holster. That is just not realistic or practical. You want to be sure that if you have young children in the house, these weapons are not accessible to them, the same as you would with your firearms. Be sure that any safe in which you keep your firearms or other weapons has quick-open features, such as a hand or fingerprint scanner, so that you are not fumbling around looking for a key in the middle of the night.

If you do not have a knife or are not comfortable buying a combat type of knife, remember that your kitchen knives can also be used for self-defense in a pinch. I know some people who are afraid of handling knives and prefer a baseball bat or a tire iron. Use whatever works for you and whatever you are comfortable using to defend yourself, but remember that most criminals who are coming to harm you or steal your supplies will most likely be using a firearm.

Self-Defense Training

Often you will hear people say things like, "I don't need to learn how to fight; I'll just shoot 'em." Those are typically people who do not truly understand how ludicrous that statement is. Most attackers will try to get the element of surprise when they attack you, and if you have no hand-to-hand combat experience or training, that person will most likely not have to worry about you drawing your pistol in time. They might even take your firearm if they got the upper hand, and you could not react quickly enough. Remember when we talked about someone with a knife being able to close the distance as far away as twenty feet? Unless you are John Wick, you had better have some hand-to-hand combat skills.

Let us say it is not an attacker who planned to come after you, but rather a disagreement you are having with someone, and things get heated very quickly. Are you just going to shoot them? I would hope not, because if they were not threatening you with a deadly weapon, you will surely go to prison if that happens. The ol' "I'd rather be judged by twelve than be carried by six" is going to sound pretty stupid if you killed someone unnecessarily and are now in prison for life surrounded by guys who are a lot more dangerous than you are. You may still get carried by six before your prison term is up. Please think before you act.

Let's get back to our scenario where you are in a heated argument with someone, and it becomes physical, and let's assume for argument's sake that you are not the guy who is going to shoot first and ask questions later. Keep in mind that most fights end up on the ground. Suppose you do not have any skills on the ground and are not trained in something like jiujitsu. In that case, you risk severe injury or even death if the other person overpowers you and decides to take it to the next level or pulls out a weapon after getting control of you on the ground.

The point is that you should learn and train in the fighting arts just as you would learn and train how to handle and shoot your firearm or how to start a fire with a Ferro rod, etc. Whether it is boxing, kickboxing, Muay Thai, jiujitsu, judo, or another effective style, you should be training these skills just as much as any other type of training. I highly recommend training in jiujitsu and other fighting disciplines such as boxing. You will want to know how to fight on the ground and on your feet. Jiujitsu is especially effective for smaller and less physically strong people who may not otherwise be able to subdue or get away from a much larger and stronger attacker.

CHAPTER 4

SHELTER

The Law of Threes

It is time to talk about shelter, which in this case will be your home, your castle. Your home protects you from cold or hot weather, so you do not have to worry about hypothermia or extreme heat, both of which are extremely dangerous and life-threatening. When I think of shelter, it reminds me of the "law of threes." The law of threes is simple in an emergency: It can take three seconds to make a life-or-death decision in some cases. In the military, we called it the "OODA loop." The OODA loop is a cycle that consists of observe, orient, decide, and act. The OODA loop was developed by John Boyd, a military strategist and Air Force colonel.

Thinking about the OODA loop will help you in your decision-making processes and situation awareness. First, you are collecting data by observing what is happening around you. Once you have observed the situation, you orient yourself and analyze the information you have gained from observation. At this point, you must choose how you will respond and act using the insights you have thus far gained from observing and orienting so that you can choose the best available response to your situation. Then finally, you must act by executing your answer to the problem. This process should be practiced diligently, and once you have become proficient, your future OODA loop decisions should become faster over time and more accurate.

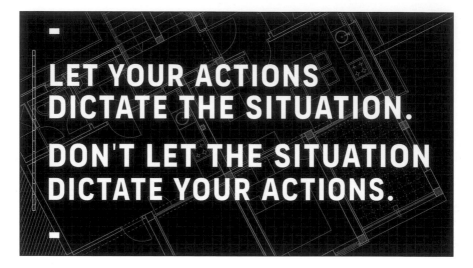

LET YOUR ACTIONS DICTATE THE SITUATION. DON'T LET THE SITUATION DICTATE YOUR ACTIONS.

The law of threes in terms of survival says that you can survive roughly three minutes without air, three hours without shelter and security in extreme temperatures or during an emergency, three days without water, and three weeks without food. Of course, these are just baseline numbers, so you should be cautious when thinking about the law of threes. These time lines can change very quickly depending on weather factors, how many calories you expend through physical activity, etc. For example, if you are stranded in subzero weather without any fire or shelter, you could die much more quickly.

What about going for three days without water? Yes, that is possible in some situations, but if you are expending calories and sweating, especially in a scorching climate, you could die in a matter of hours. According to biologists, you can lose between 1 and 1.5 liters of sweat each hour, so imagine how quickly you can become dehydrated in the wrong conditions. Water is life's blood, as I like to say. Without it, you start not thinking clearly and can start making bad decisions. Your body needs water to regulate your body temperature, and your vital organs need it to function properly or they will eventually start to shut down. Hydration is critical to keep you going.

What about food? You may often hear people talking about not carrying any food in their bug-out bags or while out on a long hike because they believe they can survive for nearly three weeks without needing to eat. I can assure you that it is not really that easy. Do not think that you do not need to take in any calories and nourishment for weeks at a time. Food is fuel, and you need it to physically do tasks, walk great distance, and stay mentally sharp.

I'm not saying it isn't possible to go for very long periods without eating, since I have done it before. What I am saying is that starvation has many factors that must be considered, like how old you are, your body weight, how much body fat content you have, what your fitness levels are, your overall health, and what is probably most important, your activity level and how many calories you are expending. You can become very weak and lethargic during starvation periods, so you must maintain your calorie intake if you plan to be helpful for anything. You want to be able to function properly in these situations and make good decisions. Also, if you aren't eating regularly, you are also not maintaining good health. You do not want to complicate your situation further by becoming ill.

Many times, I have pushed these laws and myself to their limits. You have seen me do this many times on TV while out on *Naked and Afraid* or *Dual Survival*. Yes, I get it, these are TV shows, but they are much more than that. They are very real challenges and putting myself into the challenges and testing myself does more than entertain you. Others and I have put ourselves into these situations to not only test ourselves but educate the viewers as well. I remember Kellie and I were in Tanzania, and the first major obstacle was water. We were exposed naked to the hot African savannah right off; we had only a knife, a pot, and a crummy map on hand, that's it.

We had no water nearby and had to walk five miles to get to what looked like a watering hole. We walked for hours barefoot, painfully stepping on more thorns than you'd find needles in a pincushion, taking short breaks wherever we could find shade. We eventually got close and found a nasty mudhole where the water was undrinkable but decided to at least cool off in the water and mud up to protect ourselves from the sun as we finished our hike to the actual water hole. We walked a few more hours and finally arrived at five pools of water of various sizes and animal tracks all over. We again cooled off, but we were clearly going to need to figure out how to create a primitive fire to boil the water if we were to drink it. We were so parched and dehydrated from the long, hot hike. We got our shelter together, then out of nowhere a storm popped in. Initially it was quite welcome to cool off and catch rainwater to drink. It filled little pock holes in the rocks that would be our only source of water until we got the fire going. The rain only lasted about an hour and it was gone.

We spent the next three days trying to get a fire going primitively and Kellie tried many times to do a bow drill method. After a day it was clear that method wasn't going to work, the pock holes we were using to drink were drying up, and we needed a new plan. A couple more days went by, and I was trying the fire plow method, but we were really dehydrating fast, our brains weren't working that well, and we were practically speaking in tongues. Finally, the next day we were able to get the fire going and able to start rehydrating, and it took a couple days to recover. We went five days without any significant amounts of water to practically none before we were able to get ourselves out of serious trouble.

The law of threes concerning water were clearly pushed and I can personally tell you it sucked. Try not to get yourself behind in the water department in any situation.

Power Outages

Now that we have talked about the law of threes and how that relates explicitly to your shelter situation, what happens if the power goes out, especially during the wintertime? You want to ensure that you are thinking of all these diverse scenarios. You want to protect your core body temperature when you are at home, as much as when you are out in the wilderness. Extreme heat can be just as dangerous as extreme cold, so you must be incredibly careful.

Let us say the power does go out, and it's winter. What kind of systems do you have to keep yourself warm? Do you have a backup generator, and do you have enough fuel stored? What about a solar system for backup power? Do you have a fireplace or woodstove? Do you have the right tools to chop firewood, whether inside or outside, for cooking or keeping you warm? Do you have a chain saw, an axe, or a saw? If you are in an apartment, this may not be an option, so you should be sure you have some good-quality blankets. Wool blankets are outstanding for this type of situation. Never let this situation dictate your actions; instead, let your actions dictate the situation. That means you thought of this ahead of time, and this is something that is part of your overall PACE plan.

Losing the power grid in any form, from natural disasters, terrorism, cyberattacks, solar flares, or even outdated infrastructure, can be a significant pain for those affected, especially those in urban environments, while suburban and rural folks have a lot more space and land which helps them in terms of planning and capabilities. You have to think outside the box with your survival planning should you find yourself in this kind of emergency and living in an apartment. Options for those living in an apartment, especially in a city, will depend on how long the power is out. If it's a total grid-down scenario, you really need to leave the cities, as they will become very dangerous, and your options will be very limited in terms of generating your own power.

If you cannot leave the city, you should be prepared with plenty of warm clothing and blankets, and even solar-powered generators if you have an area on the roof of your building where you can set up solar panels. Apartments are tough places to survive long term. You can set up clever storage for supplies but are limited to how long those last. An apartment doesn't always allow you to head to a river for water resupply, or ease of access to hunt or forage for food the way someone outside a city would have. If you are in an apartment, this is where having a good evacuation plan comes in.

Knowing different routes to escape the city is key—in case one is compromised, you have several other options. You need to first have a cache site or two outside the city that you can get to even by foot if need be as a hold-up spot to resupply at and prepare. At least here you can have a fire and hopefully access

to water and a chance to reset. You will need to have a final spot you are going to head to from here, whether it's with friends or family or some other location you have set up or predesignated. *NOTE: If your plan is to head to, say, a national or state park or some other campground, remember those kinds of places are on a lot of other folks' plans as well, as no one owns them.

Planning

Now is the opportune time to expand our horizons and explore innovative approaches. It is said that an ounce of prevention is worth a pound of cure, and this adage holds true when it comes to survival planning. Regardless of the emergency at hand, certain fundamental aspects require our attention: shelter, water, food, fire, medical care, self-defense, and more. While the specific details may vary depending on the situation, the underlying needs remain constant.

The importance of planning cannot be overstated, particularly when considering the well-being of ourselves and our loved ones during an impending disaster. The consequences of inadequate preparation have been evident in recent times, from the devastating impact of natural disasters to the challenges posed by the global pandemic and even the strain on supplies such as baby formula. These events serve as reminders of the criticality of proactive planning to ensure our basic needs are met and our safety secured.

So, how can we effectively plan for a power outage? This question requires us to think beyond the conventional and adopt a comprehensive approach that encompasses various aspects of our daily lives. The first step is to assess our immediate surroundings and identify potential vulnerabilities that may arise in the event of a power disruption. This could involve evaluating the availability of backup power sources, such as generators or alternative energy systems, and considering their feasibility and affordability.

Next, it is crucial to stockpile essential supplies that will sustain us during the outage. This includes ample quantities of non-perishable food items, clean drinking water, and a reliable means of purifying water if necessary. Additionally, securing adequate shelter and insulation to maintain comfortable living conditions becomes of paramount importance, especially in extreme weather conditions.

Preparing for a power outage also requires us to consider the practical aspects of daily life. How will we navigate without electricity? Are there alternative means of communication available? These questions highlight the importance of having backup plans in place, such as battery-powered devices, solar chargers, and designated meeting points for family members. Furthermore, establishing a communication network with neighbors and community members can foster a sense of support and collaboration during trying times.

While we focus on meeting our immediate needs, it is equally important to address the potential challenges that may arise in terms of healthcare and personal safety. Having a well-stocked first aid kit, access to necessary medications, and a comprehensive understanding of basic medical procedures can provide a sense of security. Moreover, developing self-defense skills or considering personal security measures may contribute to a heightened sense of safety and peace of mind.

Ultimately, the key to effective planning for a power outage lies in our ability to think critically, anticipate potential obstacles, and be proactive in our preparations. By approaching the situation with open-mindedness and creativity, we can explore a myriad of solutions that align with our specific circumstances and available resources. Remember, the power to safeguard ourselves and our loved ones lies within our hands, and by taking the necessary steps now, we can navigate any challenge that comes our way with resilience and confidence.

Shelter

Remember, your clothing is your first layer of defense in extreme temperatures, so make sure you wear the proper clothing to protect your core body temperature, whether you are in the wilderness or in your home.

Do you have sleeping bags and bivouac sacks to help keep you warm during a winter's power outage? What about plenty of extra warm clothing? Even if you live in a climate that never gets below freezing, remember what happened in Texas in early 2021 when they had that cold weather move in around February.

The cold weather froze water in the oil and gas wells, causing gas production to drop by nearly 45 percent. The icy roads caused a lot of accidents, and people died. The state was forced to ration water and propane, and power grid failures often happened. Water mains started to break, bacteria began to affect the water supplies, and nearly fifteen million people had to boil their water before being able to drink or cook with it. Hundreds of people died from hypothermia and carbon monoxide poisoning and because medical equipment was unable to function.

Let's also talk about natural disasters for a minute. Do you and your family members know where to go? If you are in a tornado

threat area, go to the basement of your home, or, if you don't have a basement, go to the center of the house to a room with no windows. You can even get in the bathtub, which is better than nothing.

Do you have a bunker you can get down to in a tornado situation? They make unique bunkers bolted to the concrete in your basement or garage that can protect you from these types of storms. If you do not have a bunker and are in a hurricane or tornado-prone area, you should investigate one of these protective bunkers.

Do you have shutters on the outside of your house? Some people who live in hurricane areas have plywood already cut and ready to install over their windows in case of a hurricane. The last thing you want is glass and debris flying through your house during a storm. No matter what the situation is, you want to be able to have a way to be adequately prepared. You must know the climate and the weather patterns that happen in your area and the things you need for your shelter to protect you and keep you and your family safe.

Your shelter is where you feel safe and becomes your base of operations. As mentioned earlier, I have advised folks in apartments that they should consider trying to get one more bedroom than they need even, though it means a little higher rent but what it gives you is a whole space that is at least 10' × 10' to use as a storage area for supplies.

Set up an excellent shelf system in the closet and throughout the room. I like to use storage containers with lids to help keep stuff organized and safe and label the contents. I also use luminous tape on the outside in the shape of letters so that when it is dark, I can see them and know what might be in each. For example, "L" is for lights. . . . that way, I can find the container easily in the dark, grab a flashlight out of it, and safely light my way.

Then start to fill it with things we will cover in the other categories. Still, the idea is to use this to ensure you have enough basics for yourself and everyone in the home to survive an extended period and helpfully get through the power grid going down longer.

You will want plenty of lighting sources on hand: camp lamps, headlamps, flashlights, and candles. You want to have enough to light up the place to operate, not needlessly, and plenty of spare batteries. If you are fortunate enough to have a balcony, I suggest having a small dual fuel (gas/propane) generator out there. If not, there are also lovely battery-operated generators that work well in apartments.

Having battery-operated fans and cooling systems on hand, though a luxury, can help make a power outage more bearable. Battery-operated fans may become critical if someone in your home has a medical condition or even if you have pets that do not do well in extreme heat, such as an Alaskan malamute or a husky. There are some cool as-seen-on-TV mini-AC units that can operate ten hours fully charged that work well.

Water

During power outages, the availability of clean water can be severely impacted, particularly during prolonged disruptions. When the power goes down, it can disrupt water flow and, in certain situations, even lead to water contamination. Having contingency plans to ensure access to safe drinking water becomes crucial. One practical solution is to have alternative methods for boiling water, such as utilizing a barbecue grill or camp stove, especially if your regular cooking stove relies on electricity rather than gas.

In addition to boiling water, it is wise to have a sufficient supply of prefilled five-gallon water jugs stored on your shelves. Having ample water on hand for everyone in your household is of utmost importance. This ensures that hydration needs are met, particularly in hot summer weather, when regulating body temperature becomes essential for proper digestion and food preparation, especially when using dehydrated or freeze-dried food rations that require additional water for rehydration.

Having backup water purifiers readily available is another wise precautionary measure. A reliable water purifying bottle, such as the Grayl GeoPress, can be invaluable during emergencies. It provides a convenient and efficient way to purify water, ensuring that any potentially harmful contaminants are filtered out and granting you access to clean drinking water.

As power outages can also result in a lack of air-conditioning, apartments and homes can quickly become unbearably hot, even with windows open. In such situations, it is vital to employ strategies to cool down the body's core temperature. One effective method is to dampen a bandanna or other cloth, wear it around your neck, or place it on your head like a hat. This simple technique can reduce your body's core temperature by approximately five degrees.

Furthermore, utilizing all available resources to conserve and maximize water usage is advisable. Consider filling up bathtubs and sinks with water as a precautionary measure. This serves multiple purposes, allowing you to practice proper hygiene and have backup water for cleaning purposes, and serves as an additional reserve for essential needs during the outage.

By incorporating these water-related measures into your preparedness plan, you can enhance your ability to withstand the challenges posed by power outages. Remember, having a sufficient and reliable water supply is vital for survival and maintaining overall health and well-being. Taking proactive steps to secure water sources and employ conservation strategies will ensure that you and your loved ones are better equipped to navigate through any prolonged power outage with confidence and resilience.

Turn to chapter 5 for even more tips and information.

Food

In times of emergency, food becomes more than just sustenance—it becomes a vital fuel source to keep you energized and
nourished. Stocking up on various types of long-term storage
foods that can sustain you throughout an extended crisis is crucial. Options such as dehydrated or freeze-dried foods and military MREs (meals ready to eat) are excellent choices due to their
extended shelf life. Most freeze-dried foods can remain viable
for up to twenty-five years, ensuring that you have access to
nourishing meals for an extended period.

When planning for emergencies, especially if you have a family, it is essential to prioritize the availability of sufficient calories
and nutrition-rich food supplies. Consider stocking up on canned
goods, dehydrated or pickled foods, and other nonperishable
items such as rice and beans. To ensure effective food rotation
and management, it is advisable to mark clearly visible expiration dates on these items using a permanent marker. By staying
organized and keeping track of expiration dates, you can ensure
that your food supplies remain fresh and safe for consumption.

If you have pets or infants, it is crucial to factor in their specific dietary needs. Make sure to have an adequate supply of

pet food and baby formula, if applicable. Each person's unique dietary concerns should be considered when planning your food stockpile, ensuring that everyone's nutritional requirements are met during an emergency.

It is essential to be mindful of perishable items in your refrigerator and freezer. In the event of a power outage, it is best to consume perishable foods first before they spoil. Using coolers with ice can temporarily preserve perishable items, but it is important to note that the ice will only last for a limited time. Therefore, it is crucial to have alternative nonperishable food options available to sustain you and your family in the absence of refrigeration.

Remember to periodically review and rotate your food stockpile to maintain freshness and make adjustments as needed. A well-thought-out emergency food plan will provide you with the peace of mind and sustenance necessary to navigate challenging circumstances with resilience and preparedness.

Turn to chapter 6 for even more tips and information.

Fire

Fire becomes a source of warmth and a means to cook your food and ensure proper nourishment. Having the necessary tools to create fire safely and efficiently is crucial for your survival preparations.

One option for cooking during emergencies is to use a propane BBQ grill or a Coleman two-burner camp stove. These portable cooking devices can provide you with a reliable source of heat to prepare meals. It is essential to have an ample supply of backup fuel canisters or cans to ensure uninterrupted cooking capabilities. Having these cooking alternatives readily available ensures that you and your family can still enjoy hot and nutritious meals even when traditional cooking methods are unavailable.

While using outdoor heaters such as propane or other fuel-based heaters can provide warmth during power outages, exercising caution and following safety guidelines is essential. Adequate ventilation is crucial when using these heaters indoors, as improper use can lead to carbon monoxide buildup and other hazardous situations.

It is important to use heaters specifically designed for indoor use and to follow the manufacturer's instructions to ensure the safety of you and your loved ones. Always prioritize the well-being of your household and take the necessary precautions to prevent accidents or fire hazards.

You can effectively address your cooking needs during emergencies by being mindful of fire safety and having the appropriate cooking equipment and fuel supplies. Remember to follow safe cooking practices, monitor ventilation, and never leave open flames unattended.

It is essential to have a fire extinguisher readily available in case of emergencies. Fires can quickly escalate and pose a significant threat to your safety and the security of your supplies. Being prepared with fire extinguishers and knowing how to use them effectively can help mitigate potential risks and protect your home and loved ones.

Other Considerations

Ensuring your medical needs are adequately covered during emergencies is of utmost importance. Stocking up on prescription medications for a few months can provide peace of mind and ensure that you and your family have access to vital medications. There are companies, such as Duration Health and Jase Medical, where you can obtain emergency prescriptions, such as antibiotics and epipens. If you have prescriptions that cannot be obtained through companies such as these, speak with your doctor and ask them if you can be prescribed extra medication for emergency preparedness. You will definitely run into this issue when it comes to certain medications, such as insulin, which you cannot obtain through the aforementioned companies. It is also essential to have a well-stocked first aid kit that includes a range of medical supplies to address various injuries and illnesses that may arise.

For individuals who rely on medical devices such as CPAP machines or oxygen tanks, it is crucial to have contingency plans in place. Consider having backup power sources, such as portable generators or battery packs, to ensure the continuous operation of these devices during power outages. It is advisable to consult with healthcare professionals and equipment providers to develop a comprehensive plan that meets your specific medical needs.

When considering security measures, it may be prudent to enhance the safety of your living space. Installing additional locks on doors and reinforcing entry points can serve as deterrents against potential intruders. However, it is crucial to strike a balance between securing your home and maintaining the ability to evacuate safely in case of emergencies. Additionally, if you choose to own a firearm for self-defense, it is essential to receive proper training, follow all applicable laws, and prioritize the safety of yourself and others.

Ultimately, comprehensive planning is the key to preparedness. Taking the necessary steps to address your medical needs, ensure fire safety, and enhance security measures will greatly contribute to your overall readiness during emergencies. By proactively considering these aspects, you can navigate through challenging situations with a greater sense of confidence and resilience.

CHAPTER 5

WATER PROCUREMENT AND FILTRATION

Water is critical; it is life's blood. The law of threes says you cannot last more than three days without water, and once environmental factors kick in, such as heat, cold, and even stress, you may become dehydrated much faster.

There are a lot of ways you can take care of your hydration. As I mentioned, you can store water in plastic jugs, such as one- and five-gallon bottles and even fifty-five-gallon drums. Many five-gallon jugs are meant to be stacked on top of each other, which will take up much less space. You can also find collapsible water containers; there are even some on the market that you can put in your bathtub and fill up with water. They even sell five-year shelf-life prepackaged water. Be sure to keep your plastic water containers out of direct sunlight, as it can cause the shelf life to become much shorter. The shelf life for water you store in containers yourself will typically have a 5-year shelf life if you've treated the water with unscented liquid chlorine bleach, or water preserver concentrate, which can be purchased specifically for treating water. If you're using liquid chlorine bleach, the EPA recommends 8 drops of 6% bleach, or 6 drops of 8.25% bleach for each gallon of water. If you do not want to keep track of how long your water storage has been sitting, I would recommend either boiling your water before drinking it or using it to prepare foods, or just use a water filter. If you are boiling or filtering, you will not need to treat the water. Keep in mind that the 5-year shelf life is just a guideline and the conditions in which you store your water will dictate how long it stays fresh. Example: if you store your water in non-food-grade containers and they sit out in the sun, bacteria may grow much more quickly. I recommend only using food-grade containers that have not been used before, and storing them in a cool, dry place.

I also recommend that if a storm is coming, you fill up all your pots, pans, and your bathtub. If you have an inflatable pool, you can also fill that up with water. Just be careful that you are not trying to drink the treated pool water, as that can be dangerous. If you purchase some fifty-five-gallon food-grade water drums, it is also a good idea to set up a rain catch system where the rainwater from your roof is stored in these water drums. If you know that a disaster is coming or that your city or town systems are having issues, it may not be a bad idea to drain your pool or hot tub and fill them with fresh water. Just remember that bacteria can and will grow in those untreated containers, so you must use a water filtration device if you drink that water.

Let us talk about PACE planning regarding water procurement and filtration. If the water is running in your home and it is safe to drink, or you are on a well-water system and the pump is still working, that is considered your primary water source. My alternate water source will be bottled water or my water storage containers, and if that water is not treated, I will use one of my water filtration devices. As my contingency, I may look to collect water from a local pond, stream, or lake and either boil or

filter that water as well. What is my emergency plan? My emergency plan will be prepackaged water that I purchase, rotate, and replace about every five years. I hope never to be down to emergency drinking water, but you must be prepared for all situations. What if there is a nuclear disaster, and you can no longer drink water from outdoor sources? Therefore proper PACE planning is essential for emergencies.

What are some of the best water filtration devices on the market? Below is a list of some great products that have been field-tested and proven very effective.

- LifeStraw is a brand with a host of different filters, including their straw, where you can drink directly from the source; their LifeStraw Family and Community devices, which filter a much more significant amount of water very quickly; and even home filters. They recently came out with a new product called the LifeStraw Max, a high-flow system requiring zero electricity, batteries, or chemicals. It removes viruses, bacteria, parasites, and even microplastics. It can provide safe drinking water

(Continued on next page)

for up to four hundred people daily, and the replaceable filter is suitable for approximately four thousand gallons.

- Grayl GeoPress—The Grayl GeoPress makes twenty-four fluid ounces of clean drinking water in about eight seconds. This filter is more of a personal filter than it is a family unit, so be sure to keep that in mind. This filter will also remove viruses, bacteria, and parasites, and its filter lasts for approximately 65 gallons/250 liters before needing to be replaced.
- The Sawyer Mini, Sawyer Squeeze, and Micro Squeeze are all excellent personal water filters, and if kept clean and adequately backflushed, they are reported to last up to 100,000 gallons. They do not filter out viruses, so please keep that in mind if you are in an area where viruses are an issue in the water supply.
- Alexapure water systems—I have heard many good things about Alexapure pro water systems. These filters use a gravity-fed system that removes viruses, bacteria, parasites, chlorine, fluoride, heavy metals, and lead. These filters have a filter capacity of around five thousand gallons. Alexapure has a high-capacity version of its filter system, which can filter up to 20,000 gallons and has four times the flow rate.

Keep in mind that you will not only need water to stay hydrated, but also to prepare food with, as well as wash your clothes and for primary hygiene purposes. You will need much more water than you probably think for these necessities. Some government agencies suggest that you store at least one gallon of water per person daily. This means that for one month, you should have at least thirty gallons of water per person to cover drinking, cooking, and basic sanitation. As we discussed earlier, this also heavily depends on the time of the year and the climate. Oral rehydration solutions (ORS) are an excellent resource to stock up on as they are specifically formulated to enhance hydration more effectively than water alone, especially in cases of dehydration caused by diarrhea, vomiting, or excessive sweating. The reason they are more efficient in rehydrating the body lies in their composition. ORS typically contain a balanced mix of electrolytes (such as sodium and potassium) and a certain amount of glucose. This combination is critical for a few reasons:

Electrolyte Balance: During dehydration, the body doesn't just lose water; it also loses electrolytes, which are essential for many bodily functions, including nerve signaling, muscle contraction, and maintaining fluid balance. ORS help replenish these lost electrolytes, restoring the body's natural balance and functionality.

Optimal Absorption: The glucose (sugar) present in ORS works synergistically with sodium to enhance the absorption of water and electrolytes in the small intestine. This process is based on the sodium-glucose cotransport mechanism, where glucose stimulates the absorption of sodium, and the osmotic balance drives water absorption along with sodium. Consequently, ORS can hydrate the body more efficiently than water alone, which lacks these essential electrolytes and glucose.

Prevention of Hyponatremia: Drinking excessive amounts of plain water during dehydration can lead to a condition called hyponatremia, where the sodium levels in the body become dangerously low. This condition can be life-threatening. By providing a balanced mix of electrolytes, ORS prevents the dilution of body fluids and maintains a healthy electrolyte level.

I remember being in the 1991 Gulf War and the days in the Arabian desert would soar to 140 degrees. We would be in full battle rattle, helmets, flak jackets, equipment belts, the works. We would get so thirsty, and it was very hard to keep all my soldiers hydrated. We had hard plastic five-gallon water cans that would

heat up to a temperature you could make coffee or hot tea with, and who wanted to drink that while working and moving on the battlefield? Water in our canteens would do the same. There were A/C cooled water buffaloes (a moveable wheeled water tanker) out there but good luck being in the infantry and finding those where we were.

So, one day I wrapped a thirty-two-ounce plastic water bottle in a burlap sandbag covering the bottle. I used paracord to wrap a netting around it to hold it in place and wetted the burlap down with water, filled the bottle with the hot water, and hung it by a carry strap where the hot desert breeze could get at it. Twenty minutes later I had cool drinking water! It was a game changer, and it is amazing how fast this technique spread among the units. Soon I saw them everywhere.

CHAPTER 6

FOOD STORAGE, COOKING, AND PREPARATION

Food is fuel. You will not be able to do a lot of tasks in a survival situation if you are not taking in enough calories. When it comes to an emergency, you will want to finish off your perishables first, especially if you can no longer go to your local supermarket for whatever reason. If the supply lines have stopped running, or there has been looting and rioting, you may have to rely on what you have in your home for food supplies, so this is another circumstance where your PACE plan is coming into play.

PACE Planning for Food Storage

The primary food source for you will be everything in your refrigerator and freezer, and like a lot of people, we do not usually store a lot of perishables that would last for more than a week or two at best. Your alternate food source will be all the items in your

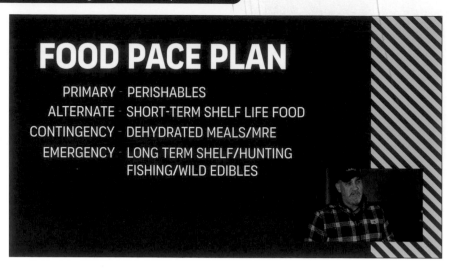

FOOD PACE PLAN

PRIMARY - PERISHABLES
ALTERNATE - SHORT-TERM SHELF LIFE FOOD
CONTINGENCY - DEHYDRATED MEALS/MRE
EMERGENCY - LONG TERM SHELF/HUNTING
FISHING/WILD EDIBLES

pantry: pasta, cereal, canned goods, etc. What is your contingency plan? Do you have long-term dehydrated or freeze-dried meals? Do you have MREs (meals ready to eat)?

MREs typically only last about five years, but most freeze-dried and dehydrated meals can last up to twenty-five years. Many good companies, such as mypatriotsupply.com, have fantastic and affordable long-term food storage options. When you are ordering long-term foods, be sure that you are paying attention to the number of calories in each meal, as well as the nutritional value. There are quite a few brands that have less expensive meals but do not have much in the way of calories.

What if you have run out of your primary, alternate, and contingency food sources? What is your emergency plan? Do you live in an area where you can have chickens? If so, you will have a steady source of eggs if things get bad. If you do not have chickens or other farm animals, do you have a garden that you keep up with to produce your vegetables? You should consider these things, and if you could create some of your food, you should.

When you are down to the emergency plans in your PACE plan, this may be when you must rely on foraging for fruits and berries in the wilderness and hunting small- and big-game animals. Learning how to forage for food and knowing how to hunt are great skills, but these are not things that will be easy to learn once you are already in a survival situation. When it comes to foraging, I highly recommend *The Forager's Guide to Wild Foods* and *The Lost Book of Herbal Remedies* by Nicole Apelian as well as *Newcomb's Wildflower Guide* by Lawrence Newcomb. *Newcomb's Wildflower Guide* is an excellent plant identification guide to help you learn more about and quickly identify almost any wildflower.

Foraging

Foraging was a skill I struggled with for years. I could never get my head around it, but I was also a meat-eating caveman. I knew foraging was precious, not just for edibles but medicinals as well, and I knew some of the basics when it came to quickly identifying certain plants for eating, but I knew I needed to advance my skill set here.

So, I started to study it as much as possible. Do not get me wrong, I am still nowhere where I need to be when it comes to foraging, but it has saved my butt on many occasions, such as the time I was on my *Naked and Afraid ALONE* Challenge in the Balkan Mountains of Bulgaria. I had light protein sources available to get after or hunt, and outside of a handful of minnows, four crawfish, and one fifteen-inch trout, I sustained myself mostly on wild edibles. Identifying wild edibles and mushrooms as well as medicinals was never my strongest survival skill set. It was always my hardest class to pay attention to, and I hadn't taken to it, as I felt the other skills were more important. But I did know that they could be very helpful and after going out on three of my *Naked and Afraid* challenges and seeing others do it with such ease made me rethink this strategy. I knew some of the more common ones most people know, such as wild berries, plantains, fruits, nuts, and a few others. Mushrooms scared the hell out of me.

Around 2015 I decided to start addressing this shortcoming. Thank God I did, because it came to bear in Bulgaria, as I stated earlier. The wild hogs in the area were mainly nocturnal and that made hunting them very difficult and they kept chewing their way out of my snare traps since the rules only allowed the use of cordage. Protein was scarce so I resorted to wild edibles. Stinging nettle is high in amino acids, protein, flavonoids, and bone-building minerals like iron, calcium, magnesium, potassium, and zinc. It was my main staple and tasted like spinach. I ate it raw and cooked and made amazing tea with it that I drank both hot and cold. I had two types of wild plums, wild apples, and berries. All safe bets. I also found walnuts, which were another huge source of protein for me. I also consumed dandelions. I learned about several other wild edibles from my local survival guide and friend, such as juniper berries, rose hips, hawthorn berries, yarrow, nettle, linden leaf and flower, elder flowers, red clover blossoms, and several other leafy greens. It was amazing, and those edibles were what saved me on this challenge to stay in the fight and make it out.

After this challenge it became an obsession for me. When I found myself in the swamps of Louisiana on a sixty-day challenge, one of my partners, Sarah, showed me how to identify oyster mushrooms and I found them particularly very easy to spot and I became a king at harvesting them. They are not only delicious but very nutritional, also providing protein, carbs, fiber, minerals, and vitamins. I ate them roasted and boiled. I now am fascinated by mushrooms and currently taking classes and practicing my mushroom skills. Please keep in mind that foraging can be dangerous if you are not familiar with mushroom species in your specific location. Many, if not most, mushroom poisonings in the United States happen because people from different continents confuse North American mushrooms with mushrooms from their areas because they look so similar. People might see a picture in a foraging book and think they've found that edible mushroom, only to find out the hard way that they were wrong. Please remember that foraging for mushrooms, fruits, and plant species should not be done if your only experience comes from books. You really need hands-on training with an instructor who is an expert in this field.

I processed acorns for headaches and pain and made pine needle tea, a staple in SERE School (survival, evasion, resistance, and escape) for vitamins. On my two *Naked and Afraid* challenges in the Amazon Jungle in Peru, I used the inner bark of the Oobose tree, called cambium, to help with cuts and purify water in my stomach, which was simply amazing. These are just two examples where foraging saved the day, and I have successfully used this knowledge in my life.

When foraging, it is also imperative to recognize the plants, fruits and berries, wildflowers, and even mushrooms specific to your area. Please do not eat any wild foods unless you are 100 percent certain that you have correctly identified those wild foods. There are a lot of lookalikes, especially in the mushroom world, so you must be careful when foraging.

An excellent way to learn more about all the plant life in your area is an app for your phone called "Picture This." With this app, you can take a picture of plants, vegetables, and trees, and the app will identify them for you. The app will show you pictures of similar plants and questions and answers asked by other users to help you learn more about each plant. The app will also give you a detailed description and the use of each plant.

This app is an excellent source of knowledge that you can implement today. Get out into the woods near you and start walking around using this app, and if you do this often, eventually, you will be able to recognize so many more plants, trees, and fruits than you ever thought possible. Technology has come a long way, so use it to your advantage while you still can because if we ever lose the power grid or the internet, these types of training tools will no longer be available.

We have all seen the shortages in baby formula recently, so you must be thinking about long-term scenarios if you have young children that rely on items such as formula. What about your pets? Do you have enough pet food to last in a long-term emergency? These are significant factors to consider and plan for now while you still have the chance.

Some of you might say, "What are the odds that I'll ever have to worry about something like this?" The odds are much better than you think. Hurricane Katrina was a stark reminder that in an emergency, you might be on your own for a while, and no one is coming to save you as fast as you think they are, if at all. Throughout history, countless major natural disasters, wars, and famines have occurred. Do not think that they will always be that okay just because things are okay now. We must try our best to become more self-reliant because when the day comes that it will be necessary, it will be too late for those who are not prepared.

How many of you go out there and see all those yellow dandelions and think they are useless weeds, and you mow them, or spray weed killer on them? My heart sinks a little bit when I see my neighbors doing that. Dandelion is a good food resource. Dandelion leaves have lots of vitamins, and you can eat the roots like carrots and even make dandelion tea from the flowers. This is just one example; there are countless other fantastic food sources; you must study to learn what they are. Get the kids involved with identifying plants; they will find it quite fun.

Food Storage

How do you store your items? It is pretty simple. First, you are going to want to pick up a few things:

- Food-grade five-gallon plastic buckets
- Mylar bags to fit inside the five-gallon buckets
- Oxygen-absorbing packets
- Impulse heat sealer to seal Mylar bags

Nowadays, you can easily pick up these items on Amazon, and they are very cost-effective. What can you store in these Mylar bags that will last more than twenty years?

- Instant coffee
- Freeze-dried fruits and vegetables (you can freeze-dry your fruits and veggies)
- Hulled or rolled oats
- Kidney beans
- Lentils
- Lima beans
- Pasta
- Powdered skimmed milk
- White rice

Are there items that can last indefinitely? Indeed, there are:

- Baking powder and baking soda
- Honey
- Salt
- Sugar

I would highly recommend researching all the different types of foods that can be stored so you fully understand each item's shelf-life capabilities. Some kinds of beans, for example, may only be suitable for five to ten years rather than twenty-five years. Always do your due diligence to ensure that you correctly store items. Are you looking to dehydrate your foods? Pick up a dehydrator. You can pick them up for anywhere from $50.00 to a few hundred dollars. A lot of money can be saved by dehydrating and storing food supplies. You can even learn about canning, which is quite popular these days.

Vitamins and Minerals

In addition to macronutrients and calories, vitamins and minerals are vital for maintaining overall health and well-being, especially during prolonged emergency situations. While food storage items can provide sustenance, it is important to understand that not all of them may contain the necessary vitamins and minerals your body requires. Therefore, conducting thorough research and carefully selecting reputable brands becomes crucial in ensuring your nutritional needs are met.

One option that I personally rely on is "Balance of Nature" fruits and vegetables. These supplements offer a convenient and reliable source of essential vitamins derived from a variety of fruits and vegetables. They provide a way to supplement your diet with vital nutrients, even when fresh produce may not be readily available. Incorporating such supplements into your emergency food supplies can help bridge any nutritional gaps and support your overall health.

When considering long-term food storage options, it is crucial to read and understand the labels and ingredient lists of the products you are purchasing. Look for items that specifically state their nutritional content, including the presence of essential vitamins and minerals. This information can guide you in selecting items that align with your dietary needs and ensure you have a well-rounded and balanced diet during an emergency situation.

To ensure the quality and reliability of the products you choose, it is important to purchase from reputable sources. Conduct thorough research, read reviews, and seek recommendations from trusted individuals or organizations. Reputable brands prioritize quality and safety in their products, providing you with peace of mind in terms of nutritional value and effectiveness.

Remember, a well-balanced diet that includes a variety of fruits, vegetables, whole grains, proteins, and healthy fats is ideal for overall health and resilience. While long-term food storage items serve as a backup, incorporating vitamin and mineral supplements from trusted brands can help ensure you meet your nutritional requirements even in challenging circumstances.

Always consult with healthcare professionals or registered dietitians to determine your specific dietary needs and the appropriate supplementation for your situation. They can offer personalized guidance based on your health condition, age, and other factors. By being proactive and well-informed about the nutritional value of the items you stock in your emergency food supplies, you can take the necessary steps to maintain your health and well-being in any situation.

Gardening/Farming/Ranching

One of the most empowering and self-sustainable approaches to food security is cultivating a garden in your own backyard. By delving into the realm of farming, ranching, or even gardening, you can harness the ability to grow your own vegetables, fruits, herbs, and spices. In fact, I encourage individuals to acquire knowledge and expertise in these areas as they form the foundation of self-sufficiency. By growing your own food, you can establish a sustainable source of nourishment year after year.

Gardening offers an array of benefits beyond simply providing fresh produce. It connects us to the earth, fosters a sense of responsibility, and allows us to embrace the cycles of nature. If you have the space and resources, I highly recommend exploring the possibility of raising animals that yield valuable food resources such as eggs and milk.

Additionally, consider keeping animals that can be raised for meat, ensuring a steady supply of protein. However, I emphasize the importance of thoroughly researching and understanding the requirements and responsibilities associated with animal husbandry.

When embarking on your gardening journey, it is essential to source heirloom seeds. By choosing heirloom seeds, you are reclaiming control over your food production, preserving the diversity of plant species, and fostering sustainable agriculture practices, as well as avoiding genetically modified plants.

Even if you lack extensive space for a traditional garden, alternative methods can still yield a bountiful harvest. Consider exploring above-the-ground gardening techniques, such as stacking tires to create vertical growing spaces. This approach maximizes your available area while providing a suitable environment for plants to thrive. Another option is the construction of a greenhouse, which extends the growing season and protects delicate plants from harsh weather conditions. With the right knowledge and preparation, a greenhouse can provide you with fresh produce for a significant portion of the year.

Hydroponic gardening has gained popularity in recent years due to its space-efficient and resource-saving nature. This innovative method allows you to grow plants vertically or horizontally, utilizing nutrient-rich water solutions instead of soil. Adopting hydroponic systems can optimize your garden's productivity and enhance your overall food production capacity.

However, it is important to approach gardening and farming with a well-thought-out plan. Educate yourself on various gardening techniques, study the unique requirements of different plant species, and practice your skills. Consider investing in educational resources, attending workshops or classes, and connecting with experienced gardeners and farmers in your community. Their guidance and insights can provide invaluable assistance as you embark on your journey toward self-sustainability.

Remember, gardening is a continuous learning process. It requires patience, dedication, and adaptability. Embrace the joy of nurturing life and reap the rewards of your efforts. By cultivating your own garden, you secure a reliable food source and foster resilience, independence, and a deep connection with nature.

Hunting, Fishing, and Trapping

I will not get into specific techniques in this book regarding hunting, fishing, or trapping. I am just laying out the framework for these skills so that you understand the full spectrum of all your options when putting together your plans and considering all your options.

What happens if you have used up all your food supplies and you are down to your emergency plans, and now you must start thinking about hunting for food? There are some passive ways to do that. You can set up humane cage traps all around your property, which come in all different sizes for catching anything from small rodents to raccoons, and even some larger animals. You can set up snare poles to catch squirrels, and you can even set up larger conibear-type traps for catching beavers, foxes, and other medium-sized animals. Please be sure that, if society is still intact, you are following all local laws on hunting and trapping, and do not use traps in residential neighborhoods that can harm cats and dogs. The last thing you want to do is find your pet stuck in a snare or conibear trap.

If you own firearms for hunting, great. Any chance of bringing home fresh meat will be a blessing to you and your family. You can also use a bow, arrow, crossbow, and slingshot. These are especially important if you are trying not to give away your location or attract unwanted attention. Remember, if you are starving and are down to hunting as your primary source of food, then other people are also in the same situation, and they might be looking to take what you just caught. Just like with firearms, if you are going to own a crossbow, a longbow, or a compound bow, please practice with these weapons often. It is not as easy as you might see on TV or in the movies.

What about fishing? Everyone loves to fish, right? Do you have fishing gear? Do you know how to clean and process fish, or have you only practiced catch and release? Get familiar with cleaning, processing, and cooking different types of fish. The same applies to hunting small, medium, and big game. Do you know how to process small game? Do you know how to butcher and then process big game? Do you know how to smoke meats to make jerky so that you are not wasting large portions of the animal? I highly encourage you to learn as many of these skills as possible!

Cooking

When it comes to preparing your food during an emergency, it is crucial to have a well-thought-out cooking plan. As we have discussed, relying on grocery stores or food delivery services may not be possible during such times. Therefore, it becomes essential to consider how you will cook the food in your long-term storage.

I vividly remember being caught in a massive ice storm in Watertown, New York. The power was out for an extended period, and those without a gas stove faced significant challenges in cooking meals. Fortunately, it was winter, allowing us to store perishable items in the cold by packing them in a cooler surrounded by snow to prevent complete freezing. We also utilized the gas stove burners to provide heat in certain parts of the house. However, it is crucial to acknowledge that relying solely on gas or electric stoves may not always be feasible in an emergency situation.

This is where PACE planning comes into play when considering alternative cooking methods. Your primary cooking source will likely be your home appliances, but it is prudent to have backup options in place. An outdoor gas or charcoal grill can serve as a viable alternative. Ensure that you have an adequate supply of propane or charcoal to sustain cooking for extended periods. In the event of propane shortages or the inability to access deliveries, having a camp stove that runs on smaller propane tanks or other alternative fuel sources can serve as a contingency plan. And, in the direst situations, relying on a good old-fashioned campfire can become your emergency cooking method.

To effectively execute your cooking plans, having the necessary tools and resources is crucial. Consider stockpiling kindling and firewood to ensure a steady supply of fuel for your outdoor cooking endeavors. If you have the space, storing dried-out firewood at your home can prove advantageous. Additionally, having tools such as a chain saw, axe, or handsaw can facilitate gathering firewood from nearby woods, should the need arise. These items were discussed in earlier chapters, highlighting their importance as part of your overall preparedness plan.

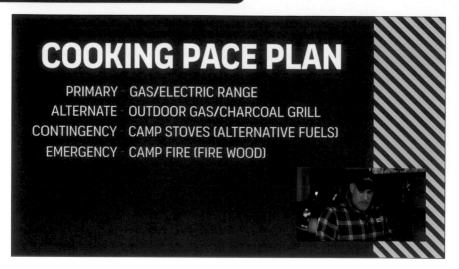

COOKING PACE PLAN

PRIMARY - GAS/ELECTRIC RANGE
ALTERNATE - OUTDOOR GAS/CHARCOAL GRILL
CONTINGENCY - CAMP STOVES (ALTERNATIVE FUELS)
EMERGENCY - CAMP FIRE (FIRE WOOD)

Investing in quality cast-iron cookware is highly recommended when cooking over an open fire. Cast-iron pots and frying pans are well-suited for outdoor campfire cooking due to their durability and even heat distribution. If you do not own a cast-iron set, now is an opportune time to acquire one. Moreover, consider obtaining or constructing a tripod to enhance your outdoor cooking experience and ensure safety.

This practical accessory allows you to suspend pots and pans above the fire, eliminating the need to reach directly into the flames while cooking. Various campfire cooking supplies, including tripods, can be found at outdoor stores, Army Navy surplus shops, and online platforms like Amazon and specialized bushcraft gear websites.

By incorporating these cooking considerations and preparations into your overall emergency plan, you can ensure that you have the means to cook your food even in the absence of traditional kitchen appliances. Adaptability and resourcefulness are key during challenging times, and alternative cooking methods and the necessary tools will empower you to maintain a sense of normalcy and nourishment for yourself and your loved ones.

CHAPTER 7

PROPER HYGIENE

It is time to talk about hygiene. We all remember when the pandemic started, how many stores were entirely out of toilet paper, right? Keeping enough toilet paper on hand is a great idea, but do not wait until everyone else buys all the available supplies. Start stocking up on hygiene products now while items are in stock.

Also, do not be afraid to use other things to clean with when you run out of TP! In the past, before toilet paper existed, they used everything from leaves, stones, sponges, towels, corn cobs, and even handfuls of straw. Fresh mullein leaves are considered the "Cadillac" of plants to wipe with if you have no other options, so if you have some mullein in your area, try it out.

In any emergency, whether you are bugging in or bugging out, hygiene is critical. When I was in the military, we had a designated area where you went to the bathroom. Those latrines had to be cleaned out often, and our only option was to burn the waste, which caused a lot of sickness and long-term illnesses, so you need to be very careful how you dispose of waste products. You can purchase portable toilets that use special plastic bags and chemicals to dispose of waste, or you can dig a trench in the ground that is between six to eight inches deep and a few feet wide. Be sure that you are staying away from water sources when you are digging a latrine. You do not want waste leaching into your local water source. The depth will vary based on the type of soil and the weather conditions but aim to dig within the top layer of soil where decomposing plant and animal material is found to help break down the waste. I also suggest using some lime powder on top of it; that will help and keep down the odor. This way your fecal matter will decompose much faster.

Hygiene is critical in keeping everyone healthy by not spreading germs, and we all know this very well since the pandemic and seeing just how crazy people were during that time. I still cannot believe we ran out of toilet paper and paper towels. For a while, hand sanitizer and bleach were almost impossible to find anywhere. Imagine a nightmare scenario, such as the US power grid going down. Very quickly, all the stores would be out of supplies, and no one would be there to restock the shelving.

Inadequate hygiene and sanitation practices can have deadly consequences. The spread of infectious diseases would become a serious problem quickly. Hundreds of thousands of people in other countries die yearly due to unsafe water conditions, lack of sanitation facilities, and improper hygiene. If the United States lost sanitation services due to a natural disaster or a major power grid failure, things would go downhill quickly. Using proper sanitation and hygiene practices reduces the spread of intestinal worms and many other deadly diseases.

Restrooms

Let us touch on PACE planning when it comes to proper sanitation. Your primary will be the toilet(s) in your house. It would be ideal if you had a septic tank and well water so that if the grid goes down, you only have to worry about powering your pump, which can be done by using solar power, and you can also hand pump if necessary. However, many people are using city water and sanitation services. They do not have a septic system, so if these services become unavailable, you would need alternate plans.

- Primary—existing toilets and sanitation services
- Alternate—RV-type toilet systems that use chemicals or a composting toilet like an outhouse
- Contingency—five-gallon buckets that have attachable toilet seats and use chemicals and sealable bags
- Emergency—using good ol' Mother Nature

Chemical toilets are an increasingly popular choice for people who do a lot of camping and even boating. These toilets use very little water, and the chemicals used help prevent disease and odor spread. While some people may be concerned about using chemicals in a toilet, most modern chemical toilets are designed to be safe and reliable.

In addition, many campgrounds and marinas now offer pump-out services for chemical toilets, making it easy to empty and clean them. As a result, chemical toilets are an excellent option for those who want to minimize their environmental impact.

When using alternate methods, such as the toilets you find in an RV, you still need to empty those tanks somewhere safe, and if you don't own an RV, you will likely be going right to the contingency plan and using the buckets and bags option. You will still need to dispose of that waste and be sure that where and how you dispose of the trash does not cause it to make its way into the groundwater or local water sources.

The last thing you want is to contaminate the water supply for everyone in the area. If the power is out and water treatment plants are not operational, then contaminated water can quickly lead to a rise in cases of dysentery and other waterborne illnesses. So, when disposing of waste during an emergency, be sure to do so in a safe way for both people and the environment. If there are no facilities to dispose of waste, particularly from an RV tank, put the waste into fifty-five-gallon plastic drums until a better solution can be found. Worst case, you empty them into 6 mil plastic bags and tie them off to be sure they are not leaching into the ground. The main point here is that you do not want waste products anywhere near your freshwater sources to contaminate them. There will always be an opportunity to get rid of it somewhere at some point.

When it comes to portable toilets, there are a lot of options to choose from. If you are looking for something lightweight and easy to grab, the various bucket toilets you can find online might be a good option. However, it is essential to ensure that it is stable enough to support your weight and size.

Most of these toilets are not designed for larger people or overly tall people, so they might not be the best option. Instead, you might want to consider something else, like a porta-potty or an outhouse. These options are usually more expensive but also more durable and stable. So, if you are looking for an alternative toilet that can accommodate your weight and size, it is probably worth spending the extra money on one of these options.

During times of crisis, it is vital to be prepared. One way to do this is to keep a supply bucket in your home filled with items you will need: refuse bags, disinfecting supplies, feminine hygiene products, and various cleaning chemicals, such as bleach, should all be included. (If you use toilet paper wipes, consider that they are terrible for a septic system or city sewers.)

That way, if you need to evacuate your home in a hurry, you will have everything you need to maintain a basic level of hygiene. Furthermore, having these supplies on hand can also help you to avoid panic-buying if there is a shortage of these items in stores. In the end, a little preparation can go a long way toward keeping you and your family safe in an emergency.

If it has come down to you pooping in the woods, do not worry. There are plenty of plants and leaves that make excellent toilet paper. Just be sure you know what you are using, and do not end up wiping your rear end with poison ivy.

You might think that urinating in the woods is perfectly okay, and if it is every so often, it will not be a problem, but over time, this can become extremely unsanitary. Some people like to dig a hole and put layers of large, medium-sized, and smaller rocks, as well as a layer of sand, at the bottom of the hole. You would then use a PVC pipe that comes out of the ground for you to urinate in. It is essentially putting together a makeshift septic system for going number one, and it is much more sanitary than just going outside on the ground.

Showers

When it comes to staying clean in an emergency, there are plenty of options if you no longer have city water flowing or a well on your property. You can purchase camp showers, which are essentially five-gallon bags that can be hung from a tree and have a built-in showerhead. If you get one with a solar heating feature, you can even take a hot shower by letting it sit in the sun for a few hours. Some of them even have temperature gauges on them.

Another option for a makeshift shower is taking five-gallon buckets and attaching PVC fittings to the bucket so you can use a showerhead instead of drilling small holes. Drilling holes does not allow you to control the water flow, so with some ingenuity, you can create a far superior shower setup for a relatively low cost.

Want to have a hot shower with the five-gallon-bucket method? Heat some water on your stove or campfire to the desired temperature, and you are all set! Just be sure you are not using boiling water. You want to make sure you are checking the temperature before you take a shower.

When it comes to taking a shower, there are a few options at your disposal. Using fifty-five-gallon drums collecting rainwater can be a fantastic washtub for you, and another option is to use a pressurized garden tank spray. However, before using this method, it is essential to ensure that the tank was not previously used to spray harmful chemicals. Another option is the sponge bath. This is an excellent option for those who want to save water. If you want to take a bath, you can head down to your local farm store and find a wide variety of relatively inexpensive basins. No matter your chosen method, you can get clean without wasting water.

I am a big fan of staying clean. For me it's more than a physical act, it's a morale boost. When you have been in combat and gone days, weeks, and even months without a shower, that can be demoralizing. It was so important that during the Gulf War, the command had our engineers set up PVC piping showers that were gravity fed from fifty-five-gallon collection drums above that would heat up from the sun by day. You definitely didn't want that first shower in the morning because the desert got cold at night and that sucker would freeze you out. Hygiene is so important, and men and women each have different hygiene concerns to address, so any time you can figure this out is huge. I remember being in Ranger school in the summer, all hot and sweaty, and the only bath I was getting that day was the garden hose and cold water. But man, I took that Ranger Bath every chance I could, and remember, your buddies and family members will thank you for it. For me it's also a meditation thing as well, getting in a shower or wading in a wild river cause that's all I had, at the end of the day, just washes the day away symbolically. For all of us that take on these survival TV challenges, I think will all agree, having somewhere to bathe is huge.

Soap

According to the Centers for Disease Control and Prevention, soap is one of the simplest and most effective ways to prevent the spread of disease. Soap can remove harmful bacteria and viruses from the skin, helping to prevent infection. Bar soap is incredibly effective in this regard, as it is cheap to buy and has no expiration date. One bar of soap for each family member each month is probably a conservative estimate if you are not being wasteful. In addition to preventing disease, soap can help keep the skin clean and free of dirt, debris, and other irritants. For all these reasons, soap is essential to any hygiene regimen.

As anyone who has shared a bar of soap knows, it is all too easy for it to become covered in bacteria and dirt. Liquid hand soap is often seen as a more hygienic choice because you are using a small amount of soap coming out of the container one at a time. Using liquid hand soap reduces the risk of spreading bacteria from one person to another. In addition, liquid hand soap tends to be used more quickly than bar soap, making it less likely to harbor bacteria over time. For these reasons, liquid hand soap is often seen as the best choice for preventing the spread of disease.

Hopefully, you have a good supply of soap that will last you a long time, but just in case you run out of soap to wash up with, here are some methods of washing up in an emergency when you are all out of soap.

Primitive Soap

The use of wood ashes to make soap dates back centuries. When lye, derived from wood ashes, is mixed with fats or oils, it undergoes a chemical reaction that produces soap. Using wood ashes to make soap is a sustainable practice that does not require using chemicals or other harmful substances. Plus, it is a great way to recycle wood ashes that would otherwise be discarded.

You will need three ingredients; wood ashes, water, and fat, which can be animal fat, lard, or oils, such as olive oil or coconut oil. Many resources are available online on how to make your own soap, including videos, blogs, and how-to manuals.

Making soap from plants is also an option. One such plant is called the yucca. Not yuca with one C, but yucca. They are two different types of plants. Yucca, as well as other plants, have what are called saponins. Saponins are a plant compound with a wide range of benefits. One of those benefits is that saponins can be used as a natural soap, making them an essential ingredient in many products we use every day.

Saponins are found in various plants but are especially abundant in beans. You can also find high concentrations of saponins in certain wild plants, which have long been used for their cleansing properties. So next time you look for a natural soap alternative, check for plants that contain saponins.

Brushing Your Teeth

One of the top five questions I get about my TV survival adventures is, "How do you brush your teeth?" I usually laugh because it is just another day in the office in the woods. I generally rough up the end of a soft wood stick and use water and charcoal. It works amazingly well and it gives you a sparkling white smile every time.

It is no secret that taking care of your teeth is essential for overall health. In addition to regular brushing and flossing, using the right toothbrush can make a big difference. While many different types of toothbrushes are on the market, you may be surprised to learn that you can make your toothbrush out of a willow bush. To do so, break off a branch and trim it to the desired size. Then, use the end of the branch to brush your teeth as you would with any other toothbrush.

The willow sap contained in the brush will help clean your teeth by removing soft tartar and stopping it from building up in your gumline, which is often the cause of cavities. Plus, this natural brushing method is much better for the environment than a conventional plastic toothbrush. So next time you need a new toothbrush, consider reaching for a willow bush instead.

Other trees that you can fray the twigs to brush your teeth with include apple and pear trees, walnut, and bay leaf. These are just a few examples among many other options available. How do you fray the end? You can chew on the end until the fibers of the twig are frayed sufficiently.

What about toothpaste? In a pinch, baking soda or activated charcoal can be used instead of toothpaste. Baking soda is abrasive, so it can help to remove plaque and stains from teeth. Activated charcoal is also effective in whitening teeth and is safe for daily use. However, it is essential to remember that neither of these substitutes should be used in place of regular dental care. Baking soda and activated charcoal can be an occasional emergency measure, but they should not replace brushing and flossing daily. Don't have any floss? Take some 550 paracord apart and use one of the seven inner strands as dental floss.

Washing Clothing

There was a time when doing the laundry was a real chore. Before the advent of automatic washing machines, people had to wash their clothes by hand. This typically involved filling a large tub with hot soapy water and then scrubbing the clothes up and down to get them clean. A washboard could be used to scrub away the stains from filthy garments. Once the clothes were clean, they would be rinsed in another tub of clean water and then wrung out by hand using a manual wringer. This could be very time-consuming and physically demanding, especially with a large family. Thankfully, those days are now behind us, but if your power goes out or your washing machine stops working, especially in an emergency, you may be back to washing clothes the "old school" way.

I ran across a cool product a while back called the WonderWash for washing clothes without electricity. This manual clothes washer uses no electricity and very little water, making it ideal for those who need alternative methods of washing clothes. You fill the washer with water, add your clothes, and turn the handle to agitate the water. Once you have finished washing, you need to wring your clothes and dry them on a clothesline. The WonderWash weighs about five pounds and is highly portable, so you can easily take it wherever you go. A product like the WonderWash is worth considering if you are looking for an eco-friendly and efficient way to do your laundry.

Keeping Your Home Clean

It is essential to clean and disinfect all your home surfaces all year round to prevent the spread of illness. Many illnesses, such as colds and flu, as well as many other viruses, can be spread through surface contact. Many people worry about getting sick as the weather gets colder and winter approaches. However, it is essential to remember that cleaning and disinfecting are always necessary, no matter which season of the year. Many illnesses can be spread through surface contact, so you need to stay vigilant.

Studies have shown that flu viruses can survive on surfaces for up to forty-eight hours. Thus, it is essential to regularly clean and disinfect areas with potential surface contact. This includes door handles, countertops, light switches, and other frequently touched surfaces. By taking these simple precautions, we can help to reduce the spread of illness and keep our homes healthy.

Alcohol, vinegar, chlorine bleach, and even a lot of the newer, more environmentally safe products are all excellent disinfectants. Alcohol has an indefinite shelf life, like vinegar, and they are both ideal disinfectants. However, they are not quite as effective as chlorine bleach. Chlorine bleach is a powerful disinfectant that is highly effective against bacteria, viruses, and fungi.

Please keep in mind, however, that chlorine bleach will start to degrade after about six months. Some studies have shown that bleach can become 20 percent less effective each year, so you need to think about storing bleach properly. Try to store bleach at fifty degrees Fahrenheit or no more than standard room temperature and keep it out of direct sunlight.

Nuclear Radiation Concerns

God forbid there is a nuclear power plant accident, or worse, a nuclear explosion or dirty bomb that goes off in your area. Do you know what to do if that happens? In a radiation emergency, taking shelter as quickly as possible is essential. The first step is to go inside and close all windows and doors. If possible, you should also turn off any fans or air conditioners that could circulate contaminated air. Once you are indoors, it is best to go to the basement or the middle of the building, as radioactive material will settle on the outside surfaces of the building. If you have a fireplace, close the damper to prevent contaminated air from entering your home.

What if you are outside during a radiation event? Anyone outside in a dusty or muddy area knows how difficult it can be to keep the dirt from spreading. The same is true for radioactive material. It is vital to remove your outer layer of clothing before entering a building, if possible. This will help to limit your radiation exposure and prevent the spread of radioactive material.

Once inside, be sure to wash the parts of your body that were exposed when you were outside. This will help to remove any radioactive material that may have settled on your skin or clothing. Finally, put on clean clothing, if possible. Taking these simple precautions can help limit your exposure to radiation and keep radioactive material from spreading. If you cannot get inside quickly, cover your mouth and nose with whatever fabrics you can to reduce taking in radioactive materials.

One of the most effective methods is to take shelter in a sturdy building. Places like schools or government buildings are often constructed with materials like concrete, masonry, and steel, which better block out ionizing radiation. In contrast, wooden houses provide very little protection from radiation. If possible, try to find a place that is underground or surrounded by thick walls. And remember, the thicker the walls, the better.

You can get potassium iodide (KI) pills to keep as part of your preparedness kits. Potassium iodide is a salt that can help protect you from radioactive iodine. Your thyroid gland is the part of your body most sensitive to radioactive iodine. Potassium iodide can help prevent your thyroid from absorbing radioactive iodine if exposed to it. KI does not provide any protection from other radioisotopes or sources of radiation, such as X-rays, gamma rays, and beta particles.

Please consult your doctor for more information on taking any pill or medication. Taking large doses of KI unnecessarily can cause severe side effects, including abdominal pain, vomiting, diarrhea, and rash. KI should never be taken without the approval of a physician. If you are ever exposed to radioactive iodine, follow the instructions of your local emergency management officials, and take the appropriate dose of KI as soon as possible.

Waste Disposal

We all know the feeling of relief when our trash is finally taken away. For most of us, it is something we do not think about too much—we just put our trash out on the curb and wait for the garbage truck to come and take it away. But what would happen if our waste were left behind? If we had no sanitation worker to take our trash away, it would quickly pile up. Not only would this be unsightly, but it would also begin to attract pests and create health hazards. In addition, the stench of rotting garbage would quickly become overwhelming.

Without our city and town garbage services running, we would be forced to find other ways to dispose of our trash. We might have to haul it to the dump or perhaps even burn it. Garbage is a disgusting yet super active breeding ground for bacteria, rodents, and even insects such as mosquitoes. Bacteria thrive in moist environments, and garbage cans provide the perfect conditions for them to multiply. In addition, insects are attracted to garbage because it provides them with a source of food.

Once an insect infestation starts, it can be challenging to control. Finally, rodents are drawn to garbage because it is an easy food source. If waste is not adequately contained, rodents can quickly become a severe problem. Not only do they pose a health risk, but they can also cause property damage. To prevent these problems, it is essential to keep garbage contained and properly disposed of.

Gardeners have long known the benefits of composting. By recycling organic waste, composting helps to improve soil health, reduce the need for chemical fertilizers, and even save money on municipal trash disposal fees. Composting is relatively simple: microorganisms break down organic matter, resulting in a nutrient-rich soil amendment that can be used to improve the planting beds in your garden. While nearly any organic material can be composted, there are a few things to keep in mind for the best results. Yard waste, like leaves and grass after a freshly mowed lawn, and kitchen scraps, like fruit and vegetable peels, are all excellent choices for your compost pile.

You can add shredded paper products and cardboard to the mix, but avoid using glossy paper or anything treated with chemicals. In addition, manure from vegetarian animals like rabbits and horses makes an excellent fertilizer, while manure from meat-eating animals should be avoided due to the risk of disease. You can turn your household waste into valuable garden soil with just a little effort.

CHAPTER 8

FIRST AID AND TRAUMA CARE

I always say that there are three things in life everyone should know how to do. One, know how to swim because it can save your life. Two, learn basic survival skills of at least the core four of survival and practice and know them well. The core four are: shelter/security, fire, water, and food. Master as many skills as possible so you can lean on them when you need to, such as how to make a tarp shelter, use a magnesium fire rod, boil water, or fish. These skills will help to keep you alive. Last, but in my book, most important, learn basic first aid because it could save your life or someone else's.

Basic First Aid

Medical PACE Plan
Primary: Your local hospital or urgent care facility
Alternate: A local community doctor or nurse

Contingency: IFAK (individual first aid kit)/medical kit
Emergency: Makeshift and primitive first aid

MEDICAL PACE PLAN

PRIMARY - HOSPITAL
ALTERNATE - COMMUNITY DOCTOR
CONTINGENCY - IFAK/MEDKIT
EMERGENCY - MAKESHIFT FIRST AID

Your local hospital or urgent care facility should be your primary plan in your PACE plan. Why? Because they have the staff and resources to handle any medical emergency, no matter how big or small. Plus, they are open 24/7, so you can always get the care you need when you need it. And if your situation is serious, they can stabilize you and transfer you to a higher level of care if necessary. So, if you are ever in a medical emergency, do not hesitate to head to your local hospital or urgent care facility—they are there to help.

You must have an alternate plan in case your primary care doctor or nurse is unavailable. A community doctor or nurse is a great alternate plan. They are usually close to where you live, so you can get to them quickly if necessary. They also may be familiar with your medical history and can provide care tailored to your needs. A community doctor or nurse can be a vital part of your PACE plan and can help you get the care you need when you need it most.

The next critical element of the PACE plan is the contingency plan, which outlines what to do if you cannot find more suitable facility or personnel. In the case of a medical emergency, for example, the contingency plan may involve using your first aid kit, or IFAK, to self-treat until you can find more suitable facility or personnel. Being prepared with a contingency plan can increase your chances of staying safe and keeping calm in an emergency.

What is your plan to cover the E in PACE (Emergency)? Some techniques can be used when there is no access to modern medical care or first aid gear. They are often simple and easy to learn but can make a huge difference in a life-threatening situation. Some examples of primitive first aid methods include creating a splint out of wood and paracord, using duct tape to hold a wound closed, or making a tourniquet out of a stick and a ripped-up T-shirt. These techniques may not be fancy, but they can mean the difference between life and death in an emergency. Let us hope you never need to employ one of these techniques.

An emergency technique used quite often, even with society still being perfectly intact, is makeshift tourniquets. A surprising number of people sustain life-threatening cuts to major arteries daily in America. Most people do not carry tourniquets with them, so I think it's worth discussing having a tourniquet in your first aid kits and on your person, whenever possible.

One of the most important things to remember when making a makeshift tourniquet is to act quickly. Every minute that passes without treatment decreases the chances of survival. To make a tourniquet, you will need a length of cloth or rope and something sturdy to use as a windlass. A windlass is a device used to tighten the tourniquet around the limb; everyday items that can be used as a windlass include sticks, pens, and belts. Once you have gathered your materials, tie the cloth or rope securely around the limb above the wound, then place the windlass in the center of the tourniquet and twist it until the bleeding ceases.

First Aid Kits

Whether you are a medical professional or simply someone who wants to be prepared for any eventuality, it is essential to have a good understanding of the available supplies. When purchasing medical supplies, always take the time to read the labels and compare different products. It is also essential to consider how many of each item you need. For example, if you are buying bandages, you may want to purchase individual bandages in addition to a package of bandages. By taking the time to understand the supplies available, you can be sure that you are prepared for anything that may come your way.

As anyone who has ever been injured knows, having a properly stocked first aid kit can be a lifesaver. However, many people do not realize that it is just as important to understand how to use the supplies in the kit as it is to have them on hand. That is why it is always a good idea to take some time to familiarize yourself with the contents of your kit before you need to use it.

Sample First Aid Kit Contents
North American Rescue Outdoor Adventure Kit
- 1 × ETD®—4 in. mini dressing × compressed gauze
- 2 × adhesive dressing—clear
- 1 × moleskin bandage (three-pack)
- 10 × bandage, 1 in. × 3 in.
- 5 × butterfly bandage
- 1 × wound closure strip (ten-pack)
- 2 × gauze pad—2 in. × 2 in.
- 3 × NAR alcohol prep pad
- 3 × antibiotic ointment
- 3 × antiseptic towelette
- 1 × IvyX Post Contact wipe
- 3 × sting and bite relief
- 1 × responder nitrile gloves, large

- 1 × triangular bandage
- 1 × hypothermia wrap, 60 in. × 96 in.
- 1 × red ChemLight, 3 in.
- 1 × mini duct tape, 2 in.
- 1 × nylon cordage, 10 ft.

Some items to consider adding to a basic first aid will be an eyewash kit, different-sized splints, an EpiPen if you need one, and an eye patch.

Make sure you know where everything is and how to use it properly. For example, most kits come with bandages of various sizes, but not everyone knows how to use them effectively. Reading the instructions on how to apply a bandage can save precious time in an emergency. Similarly, many kits come with medical tape, but not everyone knows how best to use it. Knowing how to secure a bandage properly can make all the difference in the world. So next time you are stocking your first aid kit, take some time to read the instructions on all the supplies. That way, you will be prepared for anything.

For many people, medical devices are a necessary part of everyday life. From wheelchairs to sleep apnea machines, these devices can help people to live relatively ordinary lives. However, what happens when the power goes out? This can seriously threaten people who rely on medical devices, as battery life is often limited. In the event of a power outage, it is crucial to have a plan in place for how to keep your medical devices running. This may include having extra batteries on hand or investing in a portable generator. While power outages can be disruptive for everyone, they can be especially dangerous for those who rely on medical devices. By being prepared, you can help to ensure that you and your loved ones stay safe during an outage.

Allergies can be an annoying nuisance, but for some people, they can be a severe health concern. If you suffer from allergies, protecting yourself and your health is essential. This means carrying any medication you might need.

What about your vision and hearing?. Our eyes and ears are vital for everyday life, so it is essential to take care of them. That means always keeping spare prescription glasses or contact lenses on hand. Having a second pair of eyeglasses is also a good idea if your contacts irritate your eyes. And if you wear hearing aids, be sure to bring extra batteries and clean them regularly. These simple precautions can help our senses serve us well in an emergency.

Trauma Care

Various medical training programs are available, each with its own focus and level of intensity. The ABCs (airway, breathing, circulation) is a basic level of training that covers the essentials of life support. EMT training is more advanced and teaches students how to provide care in emergencies.

Combat lifesaver training is designed for military personnel and focuses on providing care in austere and dangerous environments. It is essential to know your level of training before you attempt to provide medical care, as this will determine what kinds of procedures you can perform. If you are unsure of your level of training, it is always best to err on the side of caution and not attempt something you do not have adequate training for.

Any combat veteran will tell you that one of the most critical things on the battlefield is having good medical care. When seconds count and lives are on the line, it is crucial to have trained medical personnel who can provide the best possible care. The military has developed tactical combat casualty care or TCCC.

TCCC is a set of evidence-based guidelines for providing care in a combat environment.

TCCC focuses on providing immediate treatment and evacuation, with the goal of saving as many lives as possible. TCCC effectively reduces mortality rates in combat zones and is now being used by civilian first responders as well. In an increasingly unstable world, TCCC provides a vital lifeline for those who find themselves in the line of fire. There is also a version of care called TECC (tactical emergency casualty care), which is geared more toward civilians. You can take TECC or TCCC training courses throughout the country, and one of the best companies to take that course from is sheepdogresponse.com. There are many other great companies, so do your research.

In the event of a life-threatening injury, every second counts. That is why it is essential to know how to stop the bleeding. STOP THE BLEED is a comprehensive training course that teaches bystanders how to help in a bleeding emergency before professional help arrives. This comprehensive training program teaches everyday citizens how to help in a bleeding emergency before professional service.

A STOP THE BLEED course typically includes lectures, skills stations, and hands-on coaching and practice. Topics include using tourniquets, applying pressure with gauze, producing temporary wound coverings using ordinary materials, managing limb injuries, and helping someone choking. Some courses are even offered for free. So, do not wait for an emergency to happen; attend a STOP THE BLEED course today. Who knows, you may one day be the one who saves a life:

It was a dark, grim day with light rain in Kirkuk, Iraq. We were four months into our deployment and had been fortunate not to have suffered any significant casualties, only minor injuries. This was the second war I had been deployed to, but compared to what I faced in the '91 Gulf War, this one was much different. Sure, same country, but the battle tactics of the enemy were much different than twelve years prior, as we were fighting in and around the city. We were out making our normal battle checks when the silence in the vehicle was suddenly shattered with a call coming in over the radio, "We've been hit!" One of our platoons was driving around on patrol when they were hit by a complex ambush. An IED (improvised explosive device) went off, disabling one of the vehicles, and that explosion was followed by small arms fire. We got the coordinates and raced over. When we arrived on the scene it was very chaotic. Large plumes of smoke were billowing into the air, and soldiers were yelling "Medic!" Bullets were flying all over. The commander ordered me to get in the fight and see what was up, as he was calling in reinforcements. So off I went in a hurry. My soldiers were returning fire and pinning the enemy down and the platoon sergeant was trying to take care of the casualties. It was chaos. The platoon sergeant was a bit of a hothead and I could see that his energy would be better served in the fight, so I put my hand on his shoulder and told him, "Get in the fight! I got this! Get those bastards!" He grinned and off he went.

I quickly got to work. Medics were making their way to us but were a good ten or fifteen minutes out. When you have casualties bleeding all over, every minute counts. I started quickly assessing what the situation was; I had a young greenhorn medic already working frantically on one soldier's sucking chest wound, as other soldiers were bringing in more casualties. The medic was doing his best. I started barking orders, and several soldiers showed up. Before we deployed, I'd been adamant about medical training, not just for our medics but all soldiers, and I'd flooded the Army combat life saver course with as many soldiers as I could. It was basically an EMT course on steroids. The soldiers that arrived at the scene now had all been to the course and had their life saver bags with them. I pointed out individuals with less life-threatening injuries and told them to get to work, and the medic and I worked on the two who had been injured the worst.

The medic was handling the most serious of the injuries, while I was taking care of the other kid. He had multiple shrapnel wounds all over, but the worst was on his leg, which looked like hamburger meat at the moment. He was bleeding out profusely. I doused the wound with sterile water and cleaned it up as best I could, but the bleeding was very bad. I grabbed a tourniquet to put on it right away to stop the bleeding. The kid was doing good and was actually calm. As I was putting the tourniquet on he looked up at me and said, "Sergeant Major, am I going to lose my leg? I'd really like to dance with my wife again!" I grinned at him and said, "Not if I have something to say about it, son!" I finished the tourniquet, the bleeding stopped, and I finished dressing the wound.

About that time, one of the combat life saver soldiers came over and started working on the kid's less-life-threatening injuries. I moved to check on the medic and the sucking chest wound and the medic was doing great. He had the soldier patched and stable as could be. I slapped him on the back and told him, "Good job, son!" The field ambulances were showing up just as the firefight was dying down. We loaded the worst two wounded up first and off to the field hospital they went. The platoon sergeant ran over to me and told me they got the bastards and I grinned and said, "Good job! Take care of your boys now!" As I surveyed the scene, I felt so proud of these men and how they performed and handled that situation. I was so glad that I pushed so hard to ensure the soldiers had all the medical training and supplies they needed, because it literally saves lives. And that kid, well, he got to have that dance at our unit ball because they saved his leg. So, I would say to you that medical and health are an important pillar of the nine pillars of survival, whether in combat, the wild, or preparing at home.

Tourniquet Myths

Myth number 1: You will lose a limb using a tourniquet.

One of the most persistent stigmas surrounding tourniquet use is that applying one will almost certainly lead to limb loss. This simply is not true. While it can cause tissue damage if a tourniquet is applied for too long, the consensus is that this is only likely to occur if it is left in place for more than two hours. In most cases, a properly applied tourniquet will not cause any lasting damage. This means that, when used correctly, a tourniquet can be an essential tool for saving lives. So do not be afraid to use one if needed—it could make all the difference.

Myth number 2: You must *always* place a tourniquet "high and tight."

If you or the victim are actively under fire or have lousy visibility to the wound, the tourniquet should be placed high and tight. If you are not under fire and have good visibility on the injury, tourniquets should be placed two or three inches above the wound (not over joints).

Myth number 3: Belts make good tourniquets.

While belts can be used as tourniquets if you have no other options, they are far from ideal. Using a rag and a sturdy stick as a windlass is better than using a belt. Getting a belt tight enough to stop blood flow entirely is challenging, and using a windlass to tighten it further is almost impossible with a belt. Using a belt for a tourniquet is nearly as stupid as using a tampon for a gunshot wound.

Sample Trauma Kit Contents

North American Rescue Tactical Operator Response Kit

- 1 × nylon Bag (TORK™) REALTREE® Camo
- 1 × PVC medic cross ID Patch
- 2 × pair Bear Claw™ nitrile glove
- 1 × HyFin® vent compact chest seal twin pack
- 1 × C-A-T® (Combat Application Tourniquet®)
- 2 × s-rolled gauze (4.5 in. × 4.1 yd)
- 1 × 6 in. responder emergency trauma dressing (ETD)
- 1 × survival blanket
- 1 × responder trauma shears, large
- 1 × polycarbonate eye shield
- 1 × ChemLight, green
- 1 × mini duct tape, 2 in.

I recommend always keeping an extra tourniquet for every kit you have. If you have more advanced medical training, consider keeping a decompression needle in your kit and a hemostatic such as Combat Gauze.

CHAPTER 9

POWER

Power PACE Plan

Energy in the modern day seems to be holding everyone hostage. What I mean by that is that power drives every facet of our lives. It is the driving force to making life better, easier, and more convenient. The mere thought of it being taken away sends some people into hysteria and convulsions. Can you imagine if the grid went down how many people would panic? No cell service, no lights, food spoiling in a downed fridge. Total chaos. So, when it comes to home preparedness, planning for power is a key element of support.

In this chapter, we delve into the power PACE plan, a comprehensive strategy designed to ensure uninterrupted energy supply in various scenarios. The PACE acronym stands for primary, alternate, contingency, and emergency, outlining a tiered approach to power solutions that range from everyday sources to backup options for critical situations. We begin with the primary source, the main power grid that fuels our daily needs. Next, we explore alternate sources, focusing on the reliability of backup generators. Moving further, we discuss contingency plans involving portable generators, offering flexibility and mobility. Lastly, we cover emergency measures, where batteries and solar power come into play, providing sustainable options when other resources are unavailable. This plan is not just about having backup power; it's about preparing for any eventuality with a robust, multilayered approach to energy independence.

Primary: The main power grid
Alternate: Backup generator
Contingency: Portable generator
Emergency: Batteries and solar power

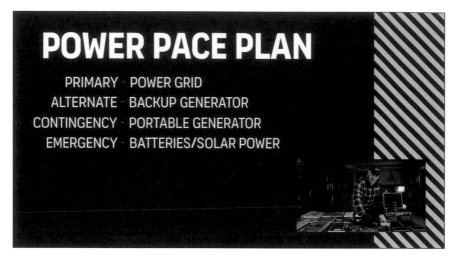

POWER PACE PLAN
PRIMARY - POWER GRID
ALTERNATE - BACKUP GENERATOR
CONTINGENCY - PORTABLE GENERATOR
EMERGENCY - BATTERIES/SOLAR POWER

There are a few things you need to consider when it comes to power. First, you need a backup plan in case the power goes out. You should have a generator or another source of energy that can keep your lights on and your fridge running. Second, you need to think about how you will recharge your devices. If the power is out, you will not be able to plug it into the wall, so you will need to have a backup plan for that as well. And finally, you need to think about how you will stay connected.

If the power is out, your internet connection will probably go down as well, so you will need to have a way to stay connected to the outside world. Power is integral to bugging in, so make sure you have a plan. A backup generator can be a lifesaver when the power goes out during a blackout. A generator serves as a reliable source of power, allowing you to keep your lights on, refrigeration systems running, and other vital electrical appliances operational. It is important to have a generator that suits your needs and can provide sufficient power to meet your requirements. However, generators need fuel to run, so it is essential to have enough on hand to last for the outage.

Gasoline, diesel, and propane are the most common fuel used for generators, but they can go wrong if they are not properly stored. Gasoline should be kept in a cool, dry place and replaced every six months. Diesel fuel can be stored for extended periods but should also be held in a cool, dark place to prevent deterioration. It is also a good idea to have a spare can or two of fuel on hand in case of leaks or spillage.

In addition to considering power generation, it is essential to address the issue of device charging during a power outage. When the electricity is down, traditional methods of charging devices through wall outlets become unavailable. To overcome this challenge, having alternative charging methods is crucial. Portable power banks, solar chargers, or even car chargers can become your lifeline, ensuring that you can recharge your devices and stay connected with the outside world.

Moreover, staying connected becomes increasingly important during an outage. While the power outage may disrupt your internet connection, there are alternative means to stay connected. Having a battery-powered or hand-cranked radio can provide access to important news updates and emergency broadcasts. Additionally, having a backup internet connection, such as a mobile hotspot or satellite internet, can enable you to stay connected to essential online resources and communicate with loved ones.

Power is a fundamental aspect of bugging in, as it allows you to maintain a sense of normalcy and functionality in your home. By having a well-thought-out plan and backup solutions in place, you can navigate power outages with confidence and ensure that you and your loved ones have the necessary resources to endure challenging times. Remember to regularly maintain your backup systems, keep an adequate fuel supply, and have alternative charging methods readily available to sustain your power needs when the grid goes down.

Potential Causes of Widespread Power Failure

Cyberattacks

The American power grid is a massive and complex system and is vulnerable to attack in many ways. One of the most severe threats comes from cyberattacks. Hackers could theoretically disable the grid by targeting its multiple control systems, causing widespread blackouts. This scenario is not as far-fetched as it may sound. Congress has been warned that such an attack is a genuine possibility.

While the government is working to defend the grid against cyberattacks, there is only so much that can be done. Larger electric companies and Congress have not done nearly enough to harden the US electric grid. The US electric grid is highly vulnerable. The best defense against this attack is to have backup power sources in place so that people can still access essential services if the grid goes down.

In the internet age, the world's interconnectedness is easy to take for granted. A click of a button can put us in instant communication with people on the other side of the globe. However, those with malicious intent can also exploit this same interconnectedness. In recent years, there have been several high-profile cyberattacks that have crippled businesses and governments. With the current conflict with Russia in Ukraine and potential conflicts with China, the danger of cyberattacks is genuine.

Massive Solar Flare

Do you remember hearing about the "Carrington Event"? In 1859, something strange happened in the sun. A massive solar storm erupted, sending a stream of charged particles hurtling toward Earth. When these particles reached our planet, they caused aurorae to light up the night sky and sparked widespread telegraph disruptions. This event, known as the Carrington Event, is the most significant solar storm in recorded history.

The Carrington Event was named after English astronomer Richard Carrington, who witnessed the geomagnetic storm of 1859 firsthand. Also known as the Great White Storm, this massive solar flare caused aurorae to appear as far south as the Caribbean. More importantly, it sparked a geomagnetic storm that wreaked havoc with technology.

Earth fell silent as telegraph communications around the world failed. The event was so powerful that it induced currents in long metal pipelines, causing them to heat up and explode. While the Carrington Event occurred before the widespread use of electricity, it served as a warning of the potential damage that could be caused by a similar storm today. Today, we are far more reliant on technology than in 1859. If another Carrington Event were to occur, it could cause widespread power outages, communication disruptions, and damage to critical infrastructure. With our reliance on technology greater than ever, a flurry of this magnitude could cause widespread blackouts and disrupt communication networks for months or even years.

Manmade EMP (Electromagnetic Pulse)

A high-altitude electromagnetic pulse (HEMP) is a burst of electromagnetic radiation that occurs when a nuclear weapon is detonated at a high altitude. The resulting energy pulse can damage or destroy electronic equipment over a large area, making it a potentially devastating weapon. HEMP attacks can be difficult to defend against, as they can target systems not well-shielded from electromagnetic radiation. While HEMP weapons

(Continued on next page)

are not widespread, they remain a serious concern for military and civilian planners. Quick action would be needed in a HEMP attack to minimize the damage and ensure critical systems remain operational.

One way to protect against a HEMP attack is to harden our electrical infrastructure against electromagnetic pulses. Hardening the grid against HEMP can be done by using protective grounding and surge suppression devices. Another way to reduce the damage from a HEMP attack is to have an emergency backup plan. This could involve using generators or other forms of backup power.

In the event of a nuclear EMP attack, one of the best ways to protect your electronic equipment and devices is to use a Faraday cage. A Faraday cage is a metal enclosure that shields against electromagnetic fields. You can build your own EMP-proof Faraday cage using items like chicken wire and aluminum foil or purchase a ready-made cage. When using a Faraday cage, be sure to line the inside with a nonconductive material like fabric or cotton balls, as this will help to absorb any electromagnetic waves. By taking steps to protect your electronics, you can ensure that you will still be able to communicate and function in the aftermath of an EMP attack.

While Faraday cages are most used to protect electronic equipment from EMPs (electromagnetic pulses), they can also be used to reduce EMF (electromagnetic field) exposure for people. For example, some people use Faraday cages to create EMF-free bedrooms, where they can sleep without being exposed to EMF radiation from electronic devices. Others use them to block out EMF signals from cell phone towers or power lines.

Backup Generators

A backup generator can be a lifesaver during a power outage. Whether you are dealing with severe weather or a downed power line, a generator can keep your lights on and your fridge running. But before you invest in a generator, you should consider a few things. First, decide what type of generator you need. Portable generators are great for small spaces like apartments, while whole-house generators can power an entire home.

Portable generators are a great way to provide power for essential items like lights and small appliances during a power outage. However, they have limitations. Most portable generators cannot provide enough power to run larger appliances like electric heaters, air conditioners, and water pumps. This can be dangerous during extended power outages, as temperatures can become extreme without heating or cooling.

Additionally, being unable to pump water can create many other problems. A permanent backup generator is a wise investment for any home as it provides the power needed to keep all appliances and systems running during an outage. Not only is this safer, but it can also save homeowners thousands of dollars in repairs and replacement costs.

Next, think about how much power you will need. Some generators only provide enough power for essentials like lights and refrigerators, while others can run multiple appliances simultaneously. Finally, consider how easy the generator is to use. Some models require manual start-up, while others start automatically when the power goes out. You can find the perfect generator for your needs with some research.

Permanent backup generators are hardwired into the home's electrical system and are triggered by a power outage signal. This means that your generator will begin supplying power to your home as soon as the power goes out—no need to move it around or set it up. This can be a significant advantage for those who rely on electric medical equipment or have food stored in a freezer or refrigeration device. In the event of a power loss, your backup generator will keep these critical appliances functioning, regardless of where you are. So, a permanent backup generator is a way to go if you want to keep your home running during a power outage.

Batteries

In an emergency, one of the most important things you can do is ensure you have a reliable light source. Flashlights and lanterns can be essential for power outages, and radios can help you stay informed about changing conditions. However, your lights and radios will be useless if you do not have fresh batteries. That is why it is essential to stock up on batteries before an emergency strikes.

Keep various sizes on hand to fit all your different devices and be sure to check the expiration dates so you know they will still work when you need them. Remember to either not keep batteries in your devices when not in use, or put non-conductive material, or tape, over each end of your batteries. This will prevent them from accidentally draining while they are in storage. By taking these simple steps, you can be sure you will have the power you need when disaster strikes.

Portable Generators

During a power outage, one of the biggest concerns is food waste. Without power, fridges and stoves are out of commission, and perishable food can quickly go wrong. This leads to wasted food and money as you will have to restock your fridge and pantry constantly. A portable generator can help prevent waste by keeping essential household appliances up and running.

With a portable generator, you can continue to cook meals and keep your fridge stocked with fresh food. In addition, a portable generator can also provide power for other essentials like lights and fans. So, if you are worried about wasting food during a power outage, investing in a portable generator is a wise choice.

Being portable is, of course, one of the essential features of a portable generator. This means you can take it wherever you want and use it however you please. It is not only great for a blackout, but if you are going on a camping trip with your family, you can bring more electronic devices with you. (But hey, what are you going camping for if you want to bring more devices?) Do not attempt to run a portable gasoline generator inside of your home as this can have deadly consequences.

Another consideration is that many people also have at-home medical devices that require power, like home hemodialysis, and a blackout could be life-threatening for people who use those kinds of machines. In short, a portable generator has many benefits, and you will find many uses for it, even if you do not know it yet.

Solar Power

Solar panels are a great way to generate electricity, but they only work when the sun shines. Wind turbines are another option, but they can be noisy and require a lot of space. Hydroelectric dams are another option, but they can be expensive to build and maintain. One way to ensure that you have a reliable backup power source is to use batteries. Batteries can be used to store electricity generated by solar panels or wind turbines, and they can also be used to power devices in the event of a power outage. While batteries can be expensive, they are a relatively low-maintenance option for ensuring that you have a reliable backup power source.

In the United States, power outages are becoming increasingly common. The United States has the highest number of power-outage minutes of most fully developed nations. This is due to several factors, including extreme weather events and an aging power grid. A solar-powered home battery system can help to alleviate some of the problems associated with power outages. Most solar-powered battery systems get replenished with solar power, removing the inconvenience, uncertainty, and expense of refueling a gas- or diesel-powered generator. With a solar-powered home battery system, you can choose how you want to use your energy without worrying about the next blackout.

Solar power is one of the cleanest, most renewable energy sources available. It does not release harmful pollutants or greenhouse gas emissions into the air and water supply, making it a much cleaner option than fossil fuels such as coal and natural gas. Home solar is also a renewable energy source that can be replenished over time. Solar panels capture sunlight and convert it into electrical energy, which can then be used to power your home. Not only is home solar a clean and renewable energy source, but it is also an efficient one. Solar panels can provide enough power for an entire household, making them an excellent option for families looking to reduce their carbon footprint.

CHAPTER 10

EMERGENCY COMMUNICATIONS

Communications is another thing in the modern day that also seems to be holding everyone hostage. Communications these days are so fast that it drives people's actions. People communicate through cell phones and emails seemingly at hyper speed. Communications have gotten to a point where you can literally get things done in minutes as compared to thirty years ago. I remember the days in the Army in the 1980s of hard lined phones and having a desk runner to send with messages to others, to where now they just send text messages. Communications have evolved so much that if the modern ways of communicating were all of a sudden gone, it might be crippling. Can you imagine how chaotic it would become if the grid went down, and communication was lost? Heck, I remember taking away my kids' cell phones for a day and you'd have thought the world ended. Communications is another area that you have to plan for, so you have plans in place to be able to communicate or take action and everyone close to you knows what that is. How are you going to get information in the event of an emergency?

In this chapter, we turn our focus to a critical aspect of preparedness: emergency communications. Central to this chapter is the communications PACE plan, an essential framework designed to ensure you stay connected under any circumstances. The acronym PACE outlines a hierarchy of communication methods, from the most common to alternatives used in more dire situations. We start with the primary means of communication, such as landlines, cell phones, and the internet, which we rely on daily. We then consider 'Alternate' methods, including CB radios, ham radios, and satellite phones, which provide valuable backups when conventional methods fail. The 'Contingency' layer introduces long-range walkie-talkies, offering a reliable option when other electronic communications are down. Lastly, we explore 'Emergency' communication methods, reverting to the most basic form—physical runners, or people who can carry messages when all else fails. This chapter not only highlights the importance of having a well-thought-out communication plan but also guides you in establishing one to ensure you're prepared for any eventuality.

Communications PACE Plan

Primary: Landline | cell phones | internet
Alternate: CB radio | ham radios | satellite phones
Contingency: Long-range walkie-talkies
Emergency: Physical runners (people who carry messages)

Cell Phones

In today's world, there are many ways to communicate with others. For some people, a landline phone is their primary means of

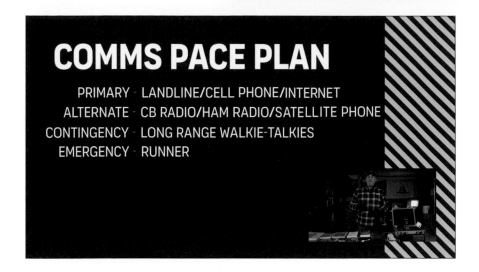

COMMS PACE PLAN

PRIMARY - LANDLINE/CELL PHONE/INTERNET
ALTERNATE - CB RADIO/HAM RADIO/SATELLITE PHONE
CONTINGENCY - LONG RANGE WALKIE-TALKIES
EMERGENCY - RUNNER

communication, while for others, it is their cell phone. In many cases, these two types of phones are interchangeable. However, there are other communication options, such as email, text messaging, and social media.

So, what happens if your cell phone service provider becomes unavailable during an emergency, or your phone no longer works? In today's world, it is hard to imagine life without our trusty cell phones. We rely on them for everything, from staying connected with loved ones to getting directions when we are lost. However, what would happen if our cell phone service suddenly became unavailable? Many people might panic, especially in the middle of an emergency.

Without being able to call for help, they would be completely cut off from the outside world. Even if our phone service did not go down completely, there is a possibility that our phones could stop working correctly. Imagine trying to make a call during a hurricane or other natural disaster only to find that your phone cannot get a signal. It is essential to have a backup plan in such a situation. Therefore, I keep stressing the importance of PACE.

Covert Communications

Learning how to communicate covertly would be more important than ever if society started breaking down, which could happen rapidly if there were a civil war, the start of World War III, a dangerous pandemic, or a large solar flare that destroyed the power grid. Lots of bad actors would be trying to take what is yours. Specific communication methods are more secure and less likely to be intercepted if you are trying to avoid detection by criminals, hackers, or even a corrupt or dangerous government. Let us briefly explore some of the most popular covert communication methods and discuss how you can use them yourself.

One popular covert communication method is steganography, which involves hiding a message within another file or message. For example, you could hide a text message in an image file before sending it to someone. Steganography is often used with other encryption methods, such as AES (advanced encryption standard) or RSA, to secure the message further. AES operates as a symmetric key algorithm, optimized for quickly encrypting and decrypting data, making it ideal for securing large volumes of information efficiently. RSA is an asymmetric approach, primarily utilized for safely exchanging keys and creating digital signatures, highlighting its significance in ensuring secure communications and document verification.

Burner phones have gotten a bad rap in recent years, thanks to their frequent use by criminals and spies in movies and TV shows. However, burner phones can be helpful for law-abiding citizens concerned about privacy. The key is to use them correctly. Burner phones are essentially prepaid cell phones that can be purchased without providing any personal information. This makes them ideal for people who want to keep their phone number private or need a temporary phone.

However, burner phones are not entirely untraceable. Calls and texts can still be traced back to the phone's IMEI number, and burner phones can easily track Wi-Fi connections. That said, there are still some ways to reduce the chances of being tracked when using a burner phone. For example, only use cash to purchase the phone, and avoid using apps that require a login (such as email or social media). Additionally, be sure to destroy the phone once you are finished with it—this will prevent anyone from accessing your data. Used correctly, burner phones can be an excellent tool for privacy-conscious individuals.

When it comes to staying in touch with friends, more and more people are turning to coded conversations using secure messaging apps. These apps offer an additional layer of protection for your messages beyond just being able to communicate privately— they are also anonymous and encrypted. The Signal app is recommended by Edward Snowden, who knows a thing or two about communications, for its strong encryption and privacy features.

WhatsApp is another popular option for coded conversations, thanks to its end-to-end encryption, ensuring only the sender and recipient can read messages. Telegram is another app that offers encrypted messaging and allows you to create "Secret

Chats" that are even more secure. Whether you are looking for privacy and security or wanting to stay in touch with friends without worrying about being monitored, coded conversations using certain messaging apps are the way to go. Whichever app you choose, be sure they use open source so third parties can verify their privacy and encryption.

Ham Radios

Ham radios, which you technically need to be licensed to operate, and you also must rely on repeaters still being active in your area, are still an excellent form of emergency communication. It is undoubtedly a steep learning curve if you have never operated a ham radio before, but it is worth learning as much as possible about these radios. There are a lot of amateur radio operators in the United States, which makes this a great resource.

Even if other members of your team are not using ham radios and you do not have anyone to communicate with, they can still be used to listen in to places like the National Guard, FEMA, the Red Cross, local and state police, and fire, and many other governmental agencies to access information about what is happening around the country.

Please be careful about trying to use a ham radio without a license. The FCC regulates ham radio use, and they take this seriously since so many government agencies use ham radio, primarily for disaster situations. There are a lot of volunteer ham radio operators, and if this is something you would like to learn more about, I would highly recommend it.

Walkie-Talkies, Shortwave Radios, and CB Radios

Walkie-talkies are the next option for communicating with others in your group. FRS, or family radio service, and GMRs (also known as general mobile radios) can be a great way to stay connected during an emergency. Don't worry about getting licensed since there isn't any broadcasting required. Remember that when buying walkie-talkies, or long-range walkie-talkies, those ranges typically do not include city areas or areas that are heavily wooded. You generally need a direct line of sight with most walkie-talkies.

Two more options in the category of unlicensed devices would be scanners and short wave radios. Scanners can pick up communications from local and state agencies, and short wave radios can pick up signals worldwide.

Scanners and shortwave radios have been a popular hobby for years, and with good reason. They offer an affordable way to listen in on various conversations, from police and fire dispatch to air traffic control and marine radio. While they do not transmit themselves, scanners and shortwave radios can be a great way to stay informed about what's happening in the world around you. And best of all, they do not require a license to operate.

What about CB radios? CB radios are most well-known due to truckers across the United States using them. They are mainly used for short-range communications, although you can communicate some long distances with an extensive enough antenna and a powerful enough system.

Storm Radios

One of the best ways to keep up with current events is to invest in a good storm weather radio. These radios are designed to keep you updated on weather conditions, even when power and cell service are down. They often come equipped with multiple ways to receive information, including AM/FM, wideband, and even NOAA weather alerts. This means you can get the information you need to make decisions, even when the world around you is in chaos.

Unlike regular radios, storm weather radios are designed to stay on the air even when power lines are down. Many models can be charged by solar power or hand crank, so they can be used even when no electricity is available. In addition, most storm weather radios also include a flashlight and USB port so they can be used for other emergency purposes. By keeping a storm weather radio on hand, you can be prepared for whatever Mother Nature throws your way.

Satellite Phones

There are a few different types of satellite phone service carriers available. The main two are Inmarsat and Iridium. While Iridium is preferred by most because of its 100 percent complete coverage across the globe, Inmarsat covers most of the world except for the far North and South poles, so unless you have plans to go to those areas, Inmarsat is good enough for your needs. It is much less expensive for the phones and the monthly plans.

Satellite phones are also not reliant on the power grid. They communicate with orbiting satellites and are not connected to traditional telephone or cell phone infrastructure. Some people say that if the grid goes down and the satellite phone carriers discontinue their service due to this, that satellite phone may become useless after time, but keep in mind that the US military uses satellite phones, so it will likely take much longer for satellite phones to become inoperable.

A more significant concern for satellite phones is a large solar flare or high-altitude EMP, which could disable satellites across the globe. However, satellite phones are still an excellent source of communication for most emergency events. Natural disasters take out standard communications, so do not get caught up in worrying about significant, worldwide catastrophic events. If those happen, your phone will be the least of your worries. Another massive benefit to a satellite phone is when you are off-grid. That could mean you are camping or hiking in a remote area, traveling in another country, or maybe you live in the middle of nowhere where cell phone service is nonexistent. Having a satellite phone in your emergency communications kit is never wrong.

Using Runners

In a world of ever-evolving technology, it is easy to forget that some of the most basic forms of communication are still in use. For example, runners often carry messages between people far apart. This method of communication has been used for centuries, and it remains an effective way to relay information quickly.

Maybe you live on a farm and send out messengers on horseback, or you are using dirt bikes to send people out for communications.

While runners may not be as fast as email or text messages, they can deliver messages accurately and without the risk of interception. In addition, runners can be used to provide messages in difficult or dangerous terrain, making them an essential tool for many military and law enforcement operations. Whether sending a message to a friend or delivering critical information in a crisis, runners remain a necessary part of our communication infrastructure.

Information

In today's world, it is easy to underestimate the importance of books. With so much information at our fingertips, it is easy to assume that books are no longer necessary. However, in a survival situation, books can be essential. They can provide vital information, from first aid to building a shelter. They can also be used as barter goods or traded for other necessary items. In a world where technology has failed, printed books can be a life-line. For this reason, it is crucial to have a good selection of survival manuals. Whether you are bugging out or hunkering down, they could be the difference between life and death.

I am a big fan of survival manuals. They are an excellent resource for anyone who wants to be prepared for anything. I have a few favorite manuals that I always keep on hand, such as the *Army Survival Handbook*, Wild Edible Guide, the SAS handbook, *Off Grid Projects Manual*, *Wild Mushroom ID and Foraging*, and *The Lost Ways*, to name a few, but I am always on the lookout for new ones. I like to find manuals that cover a lot of the same information but also have new tips and tricks that I did not know before.

It's a good idea to own a few different manuals to cross-reference data and ensure you are getting the most accurate and up-to-date information possible. Having a few other manuals is also an excellent way to ensure you have a backup in case one gets lost or damaged. Overall, I think survival manuals are essential to any survival kit, and everyone should have a few on hand. I love paper manuals because the information is always there with you to reference and isn't reliant on power to be available. It's much easier to pull out a manual in the field than pull out your laptop or handheld device and not have a signal or any power available. I store the manuals in my truck's toolbox and have in the past carried them in their own Action Packer tote, because they are that important to me.

I also keep in my survival kit these awesome foldable survival information cards that are there when you need them. They cover various things such as animal tracks, edible wild and medicinal plants, mushroom ID, traps, medical, all kinds of things. They are laminated so are protected from wet weather and that makes them easier to handle in the field. They are great quick access items to help you out without having to carry a cumbersome manual around, although the U.S. Army makes a nice pack-sized waterproof version of their complete manual. I have even seen bandannas set up with survival information on them to reference.

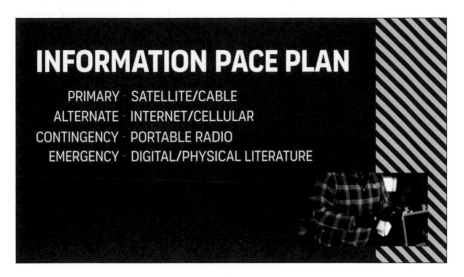

INFORMATION PACE PLAN

PRIMARY - SATELLITE/CABLE
ALTERNATE - INTERNET/CELLULAR
CONTINGENCY - PORTABLE RADIO
EMERGENCY - DIGITAL/PHYSICAL LITERATURE

Knowledge is power as they say and when it comes to survival, information is critical. While there are many great resources available, having a system for organizing the information you find most useful can be helpful. One way to do this is to create a loose-leaf binder with different sections for different topics. This way, you can easily find the information you need when you need it.

Additionally, checking in with off-grid magazines for new and updated information can be helpful. This way, you can be sure that you always have the most up-to-date information at your fingertips. By taking the time to organize your survival information, you will be better prepared for anything that comes your way. I also get a lot of magazines on the subject of survival, off-grid living, and homesteading for information and tips, and many will have diagrams and lists for projects and other things. I have a three-ring binder that I use that is categorized by survival topic and I cut out articles and place them in the binder. This creates its own manual, and I don't have to keep stacks of magazines laying around. I place every manual into its own ziplock bag to protect it.

Weather plays a critical role in both military operations and survival situations. Reading the clouds is essential for understanding what the weather will be like in the coming hours. I learned this skill when I was in the military, and it has been invaluable in both my professional and personal life. The little weather pocket guide I keep with me has been a great resource, and I have also kept a notebook of things I have learned over the years. This knowledge has been critical in both my work in the military and my personal life as an adventurer.

You can also store thousands of survival and preparedness books in PDF format on a USB thumb drive. If you have your cell phone or another device that can load files from a thumb drive and a small solar charger to keep your device charged, you can access all your manuals on the thumb drive. You do not need the internet, just a device capable of reading the files on your drives. There are quite a few sellers on eBay that sell thumb drives pre-loaded with survival manuals.

CHAPTER 11

MORALE AND ENTERTAINMENT

Morale was something that I always had to keep an eye on while I was in the army. If I let my soldiers' morale dip too low, it could lead to problems. People are getting hurt, or worse. I always had to look for declining morale and take action to boost it again. It was not always easy, but it was necessary. In combat situations, especially, low morale could be devastating. So, I am glad I could keep my finger on the pulse and keep my soldiers' morale up. It made all the difference in the world. I remember getting to Iraq in late 2004 serving in Operation Iraqi Freedom and we occupied the Kirkuk Airbase. We were starting a long twelve-month tour that later turned into fifteen. My unit was stationed at Schofield Barracks Hawaii and so we left a bright-colored and amazing paradise, just to land in a worn, weathered piece of desert. Right away that plays on the psyche. So as we went into action on our mission after several months I could see it was wearing on my troops a bit. Day in and day out, heading out of the wire, getting into small scraps and firefights, always waiting for an IED to go off, that can really start taking a toll. So, I thought I needed to give the troops a place they could escape to, even if only for five minutes. So, I got some morale funds allocated from the Command and went to work. I had an interpreter who was also an amazing painter. I had a bunch of postcards of Hawaii I brought with me for my own morale and had him paint every one of them, twelve in all, on the T Rex barriers out front of our HQ's building. These barriers protect troops from incoming artillery rockets and mortars. They are very tall and look like a T, which is why the Army nicknamed them "T Rex". I then had a local guy build an outside open-air bar complete with power and a real bar and stools. I repurposed an old pool table that was left behind, a wide-screen TV, surround-sound speakers, and a dartboard. I had brought in some extra unused freezers and refrigerators and filled them with Gatorades, water, sodas, juices, and ice cream. I filled the bar and outside area with plastic tables and chairs, had a large metal charcoal grill made, and added lighting and Christmas lights. I had my painter cut out a piece of wood in the shape of a surfboard and painted it just like the one outside of the famous Duke's Waikiki restaurant for the entry door, and voilà! Duke's Kirkuk was open. No matter what time of day it was, that place was always occupied by grateful soldiers missing home and getting a piece of aloha to help them through that time.

There are some things to consider when trying to entertain people during a bug-in situation. You should consider the age range and interests of the people with you. This will help you choose activities that everyone can enjoy. Keeping everyone entertained during a bugging-out situation can be difficult. Here are some tips to help you keep everyone's morale up.

Tips

1. Find ways to keep everyone busy, including scavenging, camp setting, or keeping watch.
2. Make sure everyone is getting enough rest. Getting enough rest is especially important if you have been on the move for a while.
3. Take time to enjoy the small things, which can be anything from cooking a meal over the campfire to telling stories around the fire.

Everyone has a unique way of coping with stress. Some people may find comfort in prayer, while others may find solace in nature or the company of loved ones. However, there are some universal truths when it comes to managing stress. One of the most important things you can do is to identify the source of your stress and develop a plan to address it. This may involve setting boundaries and communicating your needs. Additionally, it is crucial to find healthy outlets for your stress, such as exercise, journaling, or deep breathing exercises. By taking these steps, you can start to take control of your focus and improve your overall well-being.

For many people, spirituality is an essential part of life. It provides a sense of connection to something larger than oneself and offers a source of comfort and hope. While there is no one right way to be spiritual, many people find that it helps to have a designated space for spiritual practices. Your designated space can be a corner of the home where candles can be lit, and someone can say prayers, or it may be a particular spot in the garden where you can go to be alone with your thoughts. Whatever form it takes, having a dedicated space for spirituality can help you feel more connected to your beliefs and offer a place of peace and solace in times of difficulty.

Morale is integral to any group dynamic, whether at work or home. When confidence is high, people are more productive and more likely to cooperate. On the other hand, when morale is low, it can lead to conflict and division. For the head of the household or the group leader, it is essential to be aware of how everyone is feeling and to take steps to keep morale high. This means being supportive and understanding when someone is having a bad day and being upbeat. Creating a positive atmosphere can help ensure everyone in the household is happy and motivated.

Be careful about being too demanding and yelling. An emergency is already a stressful enough situation. Give everybody a little bit of a break. Everyone needs to be able to let their hair down now and then. The last thing you want is for people to check out thoroughly. That is no good. Check in with people and see how they are doing.

If you see somebody who is struggling, especially if it is one of your family members, try to help them out as much as possible. Delegate some of the tasks that are causing them stress. Take some of the load off their shoulders to focus on other things. And if you are struggling, do not be afraid to ask for help from your friends, family, or neighbors if you are part of a tight-knit

community. We are all in this together and must look out for each other. So go out there and do your best!

There is something special about spending time with family, especially when it comes to playing games together. Board games can be a great way to bond with loved ones and offer an opportunity to unplug electronic devices and connect with each other instead. Throw some good old-fashioned cards on the table and enjoy quality time together. You can even use survival cards to educate and learn new things. Whatever you do, make sure to savor this time spent with the people who matter most.

Keeping your brain active and challenged is critical, especially as you age. One way to do this is by doing puzzles, quizzes, and other activities that exercise your mind. Crossword puzzles and word searches are great for this, as they help to keep your mind sharp and focused. Coloring books and drawing can also be beneficial, as they help to promote creativity and problem-solving skills. In addition, reading books can help to improve your memory and increase your knowledge base. So, if you are looking for ways to keep your brain healthy and engaged, consider trying some of these activities.

Reading to the family is a great way to bond and have fun. It can be done as a joint event, with everyone taking turns reading aloud. Or each person can read silently to themselves and then discuss the book afterward. Either way, reading is a great way to unwind and relax together.

There are many more things that you can do to boost your morale. One of them is to do some arts and crafts. This can help to take your mind off your current situation and allow you to be creative. You may also want to consider playing music. This can help to relax you and take your mind off your current situation. If you have a list of things you need to do, try focusing on one thing at a time. This will help you to stay on track and not become overwhelmed.

A positive mindset is essential for getting through tough times. When you keep yourself positive, you never give up hope and always believe there is one more thing you can do to improve your situation. This belief motivates you to keep going even when things are tough. Additionally, surrounding yourself with positive people and pets can help to boost your morale and keep you going. Pets are especially beneficial as they provide unconditional love and support.

CONCLUSION

Being prepared for an emergency is about more than just having a stockpile of supplies. It is also about being organized and having a plan. It is important to delegate responsibilities to ensure everyone knows what to do in an emergency. This means having a clear hierarchy of authority and clear communication channels, whether that authority figure is you or someone else in your family or group.

Everyone should know what their roles are. In addition, you need to plan how you will communicate with each other in an emergency. This could mean having a designated meeting place or setting up a system of hand signals. Whatever the case may be, everyone must be on the same page. By being prepared and organized, you can help to ensure that everyone stays safe in case of an emergency.

You cannot prepare for every possible situation, but you can take charge of your preparedness. It is up to you to get yourself and your family ready for whatever might come. And if you do not, you have no one to blame but yourself. We have put this book together to help you get organized and be as prepared as possible for bugging in.

The world is unpredictable, and it pays to be prepared for anything. That is why it is essential to plan how you will respond to emergencies. But while it is crucial to have a plan, it is also necessary to be flexible. Plans can change in an instant, and you need to be able to adapt and improvise as the situation demands. The good news is that no matter what happens, your basic needs will always stay the same. Whether you are bugging in or out to the wilderness, you must focus on keeping yourself healthy, safe, and alive. So, as you develop your emergency preparedness plans, keep your core needs in mind. They may be the only thing that stays constant in a time of chaos.

Thank you for taking the time to read this book on emergency preparedness. I sincerely hope it will help you develop a well-rounded emergency plan covering all the bases. From stockpiling supplies to knowing how to contact loved ones in an emergency, I hope I have given you the tools you need to be prepared for anything. You can enhance what you have just read by picking up the Ultimate Bug-In & Home Defense Course that this book is based on at ejsnyder.com/product/Ultimate-bug-in-and-home-defense/ and hear and see the material presented in my own voice to drive home and reinforce what you have learned. I wish you the best of luck in preparing for emergencies. Stay safe out there.

—EJ "Skullcrusher" Snyder

ACKNOWLEDGMENTS

I'd like to express my gratitude and thanks to those that are honestly in this book, although maybe not mentioned themselves—their spirits are within its words. I have been blessed to have journeyed a full life, received lots of schooling and training, and had lots of wisdom and lessons imparted to me by so many. Thank you, God, for that! There are too many to name here, but I'd like to acknowledge a few.

A huge shout-out and thanks to my preparedness and survival battle buddy Jesse Wilbur and the Survival Summit for the years of support and the friendship we've developed, for partnering with me on this book, and for all your countless hours of hard work you have selflessly put into not only this book, but to me and my business. Thanks, man. I could not have done it without you.

My gratitude and thanks go out to the U.S. Army SERE School and all their professional instructors for all the knowledge, experience, and training I gained from the best in the business on all aspects of survival as a student and instructor. You all are top notch!

To all the boys of D Company, 3 Battalion 504th PIR, 82nd Airborne Division, and the Fighting Gimlets of 1–21 Infantry Gimlets whom I had the distinct honor of serving in combat with, with blood, sweat, and tears, where we formed the lifelong bond of brotherhood that only warriors would understand. I am grateful for all whom I served with in my twenty-five years in the U.S. Army, but at D Company and The Fighting Gimlets we had each other's back when lead mosquitoes abounded, so thank you!

Big thanks to my survival peer and mentor, Dave Canterbury, for his advice, mentorship, friendship, and contributions to the survival community. Dave, you have always been there for me, as a role model for me personally, and I'll never forget the conversations we've had over the years on all things preparedness and survival, and during my TV journey. Thank you!

And last but never least . . . to my family, the ones I love and cherish the most. Without your unconditional love and support, none of what I do would be possible or mean anything. You are always there for me, your continued sacrifice for me and steadfast love never go unnoticed. I have a debt of gratitude and appreciation for you that I can never express enough. I love you!

Thank you to all those whose fingerprints are on these pages. God Bless!

INDEX